Microcomputer Graphics
and
Programming Techniques

Microcomputer Graphics and Programming Techniques

Harry Katzan, Jr.

VNR VAN NOSTRAND REINHOLD COMPANY
NEW YORK   CINCINNATI   TORONTO   LONDON   MELBOURNE

Library of Congress Catalog Card Number: 81-14655
ISBN 0-442-28419-5

Manufactured in the Unites States of America

Published by Van Nostrand Reinhold Company Inc.
135 West 50th Street. New York, N. Y. 10020

Van Nostrand Reinhold
480 Latrobe Street
Melbourne, Victoria 3000, Australia

Van Nostrand Reinhold Company Limited
Molly Millars Lane
Wokingham, Berkshire, England

15 14 13 12 11 10 9 8 7 6 5 4 3

Library of Congress Cataloging in Publication Data

Katzan, Harry.
   Microcomputer graphics and programming techniques.

   Bibliography: p.
   Includes index.
   1. Computer graphics. 2. Microcomputers. I. Title.
T385.K36   001.64'43   81-14655
ISBN 0-442-28419-5

Preface

The most popular segment of the small-computer field is graphics, wherein images can be processed and stored through the use of a variety of computer hardware devices. In recent years, traditional computer graphics capability has been enhanced on several micro-computers through the use of color coding. As a result, a common interface can be made with a color monitor or TV set and color presentations can be made for business, educational, or artistic purposes. This book provides an introduction to computer graphics for small computers and covers recent advances in color coding and computer graphics technology.

The book will be of interest to persons engaged in everyday small-computer applications since the techniques inherent in computer graphics technology are common to most applications. Typical areas of major small-computer applications are:

- Engineering design
- Personal/home computing
- Data processing for small business
- Education
- Scientific analysis
- Business analysis

Graphics technology is inexpensive and is included in many small computers as part of the total systems package. This book tells how to use this valuable resource.

Microcomputer Graphics and Programming Techniques is complete and covers everything a person needs to know to do computer graphics. Topics covered in the book include:

- Basic computer concepts
- Modern graphics technology

- Graphics programming
- Low-resolution computer graphics
- High-resolution computer graphics
- Color coding
- 3-D computer graphics
- Projection techniques
- Rotation and presentation

Inherent in the above list of topics is the objective of the book: *to familiarize the reader with modern graphics technology*. After reading the book, a person should be able to do the following:

- Understand basic computer concepts and programming
- Understand computer graphics techniques
- Be able to write a computer graphics program using low-resolution or high-resolution graphics
- Enhance an image using color coding
- Understand projection and rotation

The subject matter of the book, the textual material, and the programs themselves have been class tested with architecture, art, design, and other fine arts students at Pratt Institute in New York. However, the usefulness of the book is not limited to the classroom. Small-computer graphics is of general interest to the professional person and to lay persons alike.

The book is complete with illustrations, examples, and listings of actual graphics programs. In fact, the book contains over 20 practical graphics programs worth several hundred dollars.

To a large extent, this book is a tribute to the small-computer field and the exciting world of microcomputers. The programs were written for and run on an Apple II Plus microcomputer system. Moreover, each program was "picked over" and understood by many students with nontechnical backgrounds. And that's progress.

It is a pleasure to acknowledge the cooperation of my wife Margaret who assisted with manuscript preparation.

Harry Katzan, Jr.

Contents

1

Introduction to Small-Computer Graphics

One of the most popular applications of small computers is graphics, wherein a person with the assistance of a computer is able to generate visual images for business analysis, for artistic design, for entertainment, or for science and engineering purposes. Intertwined with the above applications is the educational dimension of small computers wherein the "computer in the classroom" can be used to augment traditional teaching methods. Through the use of computer graphics, all aspects of computer-assisted instruction, data analysis, and problem solving can be made more meaningful when information is presented in a visual form. Computer graphics has been used with architectural presentations, advertising, and even sports. The overall impact of a computer graphics presentation can be very great even though the level of sophistication of the computer technology employed is relatively low. Thus, a business person, designer, engineer, teacher, artist – to represent only a few professions – can effectively use computer graphics without being a computer expert. The objective of this book, therefore, is to present the subject matter of computer graphics in such a manner that it is accessible to the person who is definitely not a computer specialist.

THE COMPUTER ENVIRONMENT

The computer environment for this book is the small computer that can be purchased at a computer store. Two popular names for equipment of this type are the personal computer and the home computer.

Some typical computers in this class are the Apple™, the TRS-80™, the Atari™, and the PET™. As computers go, these machines are relatively inexpensive, ranging in price from $500 to $6000. These limits are given only for informational purposes. Also, several computers in this class have more expensive counterparts intended primarily for small-business applications. The information presented in this book applies to these "larger" computers as well, since they almost always contain computer graphics facilities.

Even though modern small computers are not expensive, they are powerful. In fact, a computer about the size of an ordinary office typewriter has approximately the same computing power as a room full of computing equipment had only 20 years ago.

The small computer to which we are referring can be properly classed as a *microcomputer*. Some people refer to these computers as microprocessors, but to be perfectly accurate here, it is important to note that the term *microprocessor* denotes only the processing element of a microcomputer system, and not the other components of the system such as memory, display, and printer. In addition to covering computer graphics, this book also introduces modern computer technology. Full comprehension of the computer words is not necessary at this point.

This book has a natural orientation to microcomputers, but the computer graphics techniques that are presented are not limited to this class of computers. The methods apply equally well to larger computers, normally classed as small-business computers, minicomputers, medium-sized computers, and large computers.

Many microcomputers have the capability for color coding, so that multicolored visual images can be generated. In general, the methods of computer graphics apply equally well to black-and-white displays and color displays. The capability for generating color is a characteristic of the computer. However, a "color" device, such as a color TV set or a color monitor, is additionally needed to display a multicolored image.

TYPICAL GRAPHICS SYSTEMS

In order to do computer graphics, a person needs a computer and a display device, such as the system shown in Figure 1.1. The display device is usually an ordinary TV set or a special device known as a

Figure 1.1 Home/personal computer system. (Courtesy Apple Computer Inc.)

display monitor. The computer is normally housed in the keyboard unit that contains the microprocessor, the memory, and the control circuitry of the computer. The keyboard is used for data entry, and output appears in textual or visual form on the screen. This description gives a minimum configuration. In order to store information, a tape cassette unit or a disk unit is needed. For hard-copy output, a printer is needed. Figure 1.2 depicts a more comprehensive computer graphics system within the "small-computer" domain.

The equipment covered above constitutes only the hardware of the system. Another ingredient that is needed in a graphics system is *software* − a term taken collectively to denote the commands and

Figure 1.2 Microcomputer system. (Courtesy Apple Computer Inc.)

instructions that control the operation of the computer. In order to do small-computer graphics, you need both hardware and software.

Simple commands entered at the keyboard permit a person to do elementary computer graphics, but the results are not very dramatic. In fact, this chapter contains an example of a visual image generated only by commands entered at the keyboard. More complex images require the use of a *program,* which is an ordered collection of computer instructions. When the computer instructions are executed, a visual image is generated on the screen.

Graphics programs can be obtained in one of two general ways: A person can write his or her own program or a program can be obtained from an outside source. In order to make your own program, a knowledge of basic graphics technology and of computer programming methods is needed. The objective of this book is to supply both types of information. When a program is obtained from an outside source, it is either purchased, leased, borrowed, or received free of charge. Programs in the latter category tend to be more sophisticated because they are developed for widespread distribution. Although some knowledge of graphics technology is needed to use a "packaged" program, it is usually less than is needed to actually develop the program. Some of the names commonly associated with packaged programs for small-computer graphics are "the electric crayon," "the computer paintbrush," and so forth.

FAMILIAR APPLICATIONS OF COMPUTER GRAPHICS

Computer graphics applications for medium to large computers are very complex and very sophisticated in advanced technological developments. This field is for specialists normally concerned with military and industrial control activities. For example, advanced graphics techniques are commonly employed with military and space systems, transportation systems, and energy management. Most of us have seen in real life or in the movies or on television large control rooms in which graphics displays are being used to monitor some sort of complex activity.

Small-computer graphics does not require a high degree of specialization and is frequently used in advertising, business presentations, games, engineering and science, and education. A common example of small computer graphics would be a television advertisement wherein a multicolored image, such as a human face, is generated by a computer as a collage of reasonably small rectangles — each of which can be individually color coded. This is an example of "low-resolution" graphics.

In a business presentation, data are conveniently displayed as a "pie chart" or as a frequency histogram. When graphic information is displayed as a collection of lines and points, as compared to rectangles, the technique is known as "high-resolution" graphics. This book introduces both low-resolution and high-resolution graphics.

In education, for example, the presentation of simple arithmetic can be enhanced by using visual images for the pupil to manipulate, such as adding two baseballs to three baseballs and then generating, in one form or another, a result of five baseballs. Computer games are commonplace and usually involve an interchange between the user and the computer for manipulation of moving visual objects such as automobiles, space ships, and Ping-Pong balls. In engineering and science, microcomputers are connected to laboratory devices and results are displayed in graphic form.

Figure 1.3 shows an assortment of small-computer graphic images.

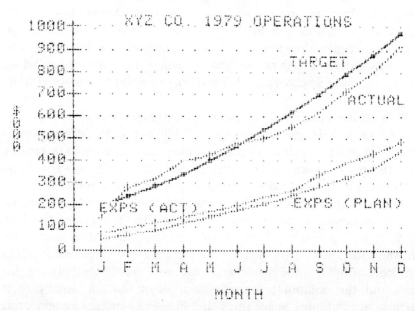

Figure 1.3 Assortment of small-computer graphic images.

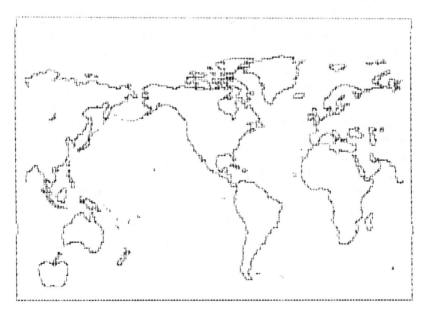

Figure 1.3 (Continued)

THE GRAPHICS SCREEN

Since the device used to display computer graphics can in fact be a television screen, it is feasible to conceptualize the graphics screen as an ordinary television set. However, in some cases, the graphics screen is a black-and-white or color monitor device. In all cases, the result is practically the same. In order to put information on the screen, it is necessary to specify where the information should be placed. With most display systems, three modes are available: text mode, low-resolution mode, and high-resolution mode. Some graphics systems do not provide all three modes and others combine them to some degree. It is useful to cover them separately here. As explained later in this section, nominal values are given for the size of the screen, under the assumption that it is always better to deal with concrete ideas.

Text Mode

In the text mode, the screen can be used to display 24 lines of characters with each line containing up to 40 characters. Each character is formed from a dot matrix that is five dots wide and seven dots high. There is a one-dot space on each side of the character and a one-dot line above each line of characters. Effectively, each character occupies a position on the screen that is seven dots wide and eight dots high. Figure 1.4 gives the 5 X 7-dot matrices for the commonly used computer characters. The text mode is used for the display of textual information, such as programs, reports, instructions, options, and operational menus.

The line positions on the screen are numbered 1 through 24, where line position 1 is on the top and line position 24 is on the bottom. Figure 1.5 gives a map of the text screen. The user normally does not have to be concerned with screen line positions when displaying textual information. Lines are displayed one below another until the screen is full. Then, the contents of the screen scroll up one line position as each additional line is added at the bottom. When text is combined with graphics, screen position is significant, and that is where the line position is used.

Figure 1.4 Commonly-used characters represented as 5×7 dot matrices.

Low-Resolution Graphics Mode

In the low-resolution graphics mode, the screen is divided into 40 rows and 40 columns. At the intersection of each row and each column is a small rectangle. Low-resolution graphics consists of lighting up the appropriate rectangles to create the desired visual image. It is also possible to specify the color of each rectangle so that a colored image can be displayed if the screen permits it. Figure 1.6 gives a schematic of the low-resolution screen. As is easily noticed, the columns are numbered 0 through 39, and the rows are numbered 0 through 39 as well.

There is a correspondence between low-resolution rectangles and characters in the text mode. In particular, each character position

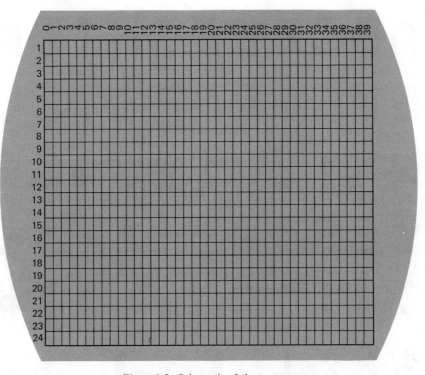

Figure 1.5   Schematic of the text screen.

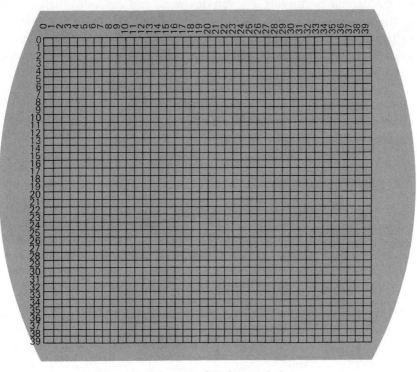

Figure 1.6   Schematic of the low-resolution screen.

on the screen occupying a seven-dot-wide and eight-dot-high matrix in the text mode is used to represent two colored rectangles stacked vertically in the character position in the low-resolution graphics mode. It follows that each low-resolution rectangle is seven dots wide and four dots high, thus, 20 rows of left character positions can represent 40 rows of low-resolution rectangles. The correspondence between text and low-resolution modes effectively yields the 40 X 40 size of the low-resolution screen with four rows left on the bottom for textual information.

High-Resolution Graphics Mode

In the high-resolution graphics mode, an image is generated on the screen as an arrangement of dots. The term *high resolution* stems from the fact that greater visual fidelity can be obtained through dots than with small rectangles.

In the high-resolution graphics mode, the screen is regarded as a matrix 280 dots wide and either 160 or 192 dots high. The rows are numbered 0 through 159 or 0 through 191, and the columns are numbered 0 through 279. High-resolution graphics consists of lighting up the appropriate dots to create the desired visual image. As with low-resolution graphics, screen positions are numbered from left to right and from top to bottom.

When high-resolution graphics is used, an image is generated through an arrangement of dots. A line, circle, or any other object is comprised of dots placed appropriately close to one another.

With a "small" high-resolution graphics screen, that is, one with 160 rows, the bottom four rows of the screen can be used for text. With the "full" high-resolution screen, the 192 rows occupy the complete screen. Figure 1.7 gives an example of a high-resolution image demonstrating the composition of dots in a meaningful pattern.

Screen Specifications

The specifications given above for the graphics screen were arbitrarily selected as being representative of existing small computers with graphics capability. Clearly, the same principles apply to graphics technology in general, regardless of the exact specifications of the screen or of a particular computer. Interested readers can easily trans-

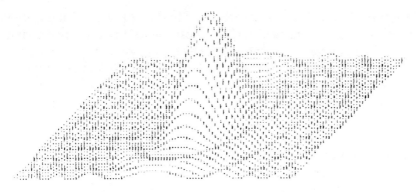

Figure 1.7   Example of a high-resolution image.

late the attributes to suit their specific needs. The same philosophy applies to graphics commands given in this and later chapters. One set of methods is presented in this book for producing graphics images. Similar methods are available for other computers, such that the translation factor is minimal.

THE KEYBOARD

The keyboard is an integral part of a small-computer system, since it is the user's primary means of entering information into the system.

Figure 1.8 is a schematic of a typical computer keyboard. The first point to notice about it is that the keys are similar to those of an ordi-

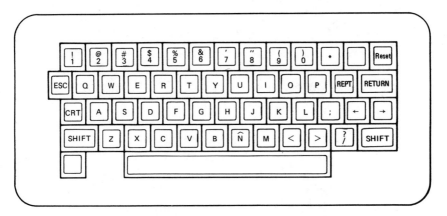

Figure 1.8   Schematic of a typical computer keyboard.

nary typewriter. There are two aspects to this: (1) The meaning of the various keys are the same, and (2) the positions of the keys are the same. The primary difference between a typewriter keyboard and a computer keyboard is that there are special keys on the computer keyboard, such as RESET, REPT, ESC, and CTRL. These keys are used to assist in operating the computer and are not covered further in this book. Each computer uses these special keys in its own way.

The RETURN key on the computer is analogous to that on a type-writer. With an electric typewriter, the RETURN key is used to "return" the carriage to its leftmost position. There is no carriage with a keyboard/display unit, so the position in a line is denoted by a flashing cursor. With a computer keyboard, therefore, the RETURN key moves the flashing cursor to the leftmost position in the next line. An additional action takes place with the computer. When the RETURN key is pressed, the contents of the current line, i.e., the line in which the cursor is present, is entered into the computer as an input line.

Now, what the computer does with the input line depends upon the mode that it is in and the contents of the line. The important point to remember is, of course, that the keyboard is used as an ordinary electric typewriter.

INPUT LINES, COMMANDS, AND PROGRAMS

When an input line is entered into the computer, it can represent one of several things:

- A command to the computer system
- A statement to be executed immediately
- A statement to be saved as part of a program that will be executed later
- A specification of one or more items of information that are used by an executing program

Each type of input will be discussed separately, but first, it is useful to cover the various operational modes of the computer. Some notes on terminology are necessary. A command to the computer is just that. It is a series of one or more words that literally "order" the computer to do something. When it is required that programming of the computer must be done, then a special language is needed to facilitate programming. In this book, the BASIC language is used for graphics programming. Input to the computer in the BASIC language is comprised of statements, so a program consists of a series of statements. Frequently a statement in BASIC is entered for immediate execution.

Operational Modes of the Computer

A small graphics computer operates in three modes:

- The command mode
- The program mode
- The execution mode

In the *command mode*, commands to the computer or immediate statements are processed when they are entered. In the *program mode*, statements are saved as part of a program for subsequent execution. In the *execution mode*, a program is processed by the computer on a statement-by-statement basis. The operation of a graphics computer is depicted in Figure 1.9, which illustrates the manner in which control passes among the three modes in response to various forms of input. Clearly, this diagram is a simplification of the internal functioning of a computer system, but it does serve to emphasize the important fact that a computer operates in well-defined and predictable patterns. As the user enters lines into the computer, it passes between the various modes automatically. In most cases, it is not even necessary to think about the various modes. There are times, however, when it is important to think about the modes in order to understand why the computer responded in the manner in which it did.

Command Mode

The primary objective of the command mode is to control the operation of the computer system by recognizing predefined words (such as RUN and LIST) and executing corresponding sequences of

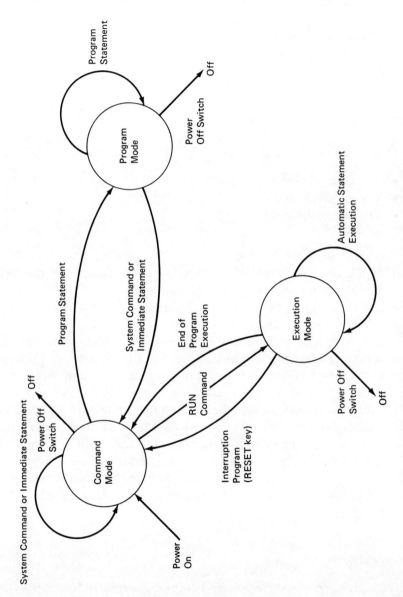

Figure 1.9 Operational modes of the computer in response to various forms of input.

computer instructions that are "built in" to the software of the system. Typical commands are:

Command	Description
RUN	Commands the computer to execute (i.e., to "run") a program
NEW	Commands the computer to "clear out" the old program as a new one will be entered
LIST	Commands the computer to display a program on the screen

A command is entered by the user as an input line, and the computer responds immediately by performing the requested function. For example, if the user entered the word:

RUN

and then pressed the RETUF.N key, the computer would execute the program currently residing in its memory. Similarly, if the user entered the word:

LIST

and then pressed the RETURN key, the computer would respond by displaying the program in its memory on a line-by-line basis.

Closely related to the notion of a command in the sense of immediate execution is the *immediate statement,* which is a series of one or more computer instructions written in a computer language, such as BASIC. Typical immediate statements are:

PRINT 36+50

which displays a result of 86, and

A=5937

which assigns the value of 5937 to the variable names A. Then if the user entered:

PRINT A

the computer would respond with a value of 5937. As with a command, an immediate statement is entered by the user as an input line and the computer always responds immediately with the computed result.

Program Mode

In the *program mode,* statements are saved as part of a program to be subsequently executed with the RUN command. A reasonably straightforward example of a computer program, entered in the program mode, is

```
10 INPUT A,B
20 C=A+B
30 PRINT C
```

This program is composed of three statements, each prefixed by a statement number. It is the presence of the statement number that denotes the program mode. When the computer detects the presence of the statement number, it saves the statement as part of a program. In addition to denoting the program mode, the statement number is used to put the statements in the desired sequence. This leads to the key distinction between an immediate statement and a statement that is part of a program. It is simply the statement number. If a statement has a statement number in front of it, then it is stored in the computer's memory as a statement in a program. If it has no statement number, it is executed immediately.

Execution Mode

The computer goes into the execution mode when a RUN command is entered. Note here that in Figure 1.9, an arrow runs from the "command mode" to the "execution mode" and it is labeled accordingly.

Consider the following sequence of input lines (to the computer):

	10 INPUT A,B	(1)
	20 C=A+B	(2)
Input to the	30 PRINT C	(3)
computer	RUN	(4)
	? 3,2	(5)

Output from the computer	5

Input lines (1) through (3) are the program. Statement numbered 10, that is,

10 INPUT A,B

tells the computer to expect two values from the user: A and B. Moreover, the numbers should be assigned to variables A and B. Statement numbered 20 tells the computer to add A and B and put the result in C. Statement numbered 30 tells the computer to print the value of C. That is the program.

Line (4) is the RUN command, which puts the computer in the execution mode and begins execution of the program. The first statement the computer comes to is the INPUT statement, so the question mark (?) is displayed so that the user knows it is time to enter something. In this case, the values 3 and 2 are entered, separated by a comma. The computer then goes on to the next statement that computes C. Finally, the result is printed, and that is where the output value of 5 comes from.

To summarize briefly, statements for a program are stored until a RUN command is entered. Only at that time is the program actually executed.

GRAPHICS IN THE IMMEDIATE MODE

Computer graphics can be done in either the immediate mode or the program mode. The result is the same, but the immediate mode is cumbersome when the visual image is complicated and the number of statements is large.

Frames

In order to get the feel of what we are about to do, consider the sequence of frames given in Figure 1.10. They simply depict the screen as statements are entered in the immediate mode. Of course, the screen really holds 24 lines, but the result is obviously the same. It is important to note that anything enclosed in quotation marks is taken literally, as is, whereas numbers are truly regarded as numbers. Also, the HOME command clears the screen and moves the flashing cursor, which indicates the position of the next input character, to the upper left screen position. Figure 1.11 gives another sequence of frames representing some calculations. In the latter figure, you will detect the asterisk symbol, which represents multiplication.

Low-Resolution Graphics Mode

In order to do graphics on the computer, you must first put the computer in the graphics mode. For low-resolution graphics, this is accomplished by typing the GR statement as follows:

GR

and then pressing the RETURN key. When this command is received by the computer, the screen is cleared and the low-resolution graphics mode is entered. In this mode, only the bottom four lines of the screen are used for text. Above the text is a 40 X 40 matrix of rectangles that can be illuminated with graphics instructions.

In order to illuminate a rectangle, the computer needs two items of information:

1. The color of the rectangle
2. The location of the rectangle

To set the color, enter a statement of the form:

COLOR = n

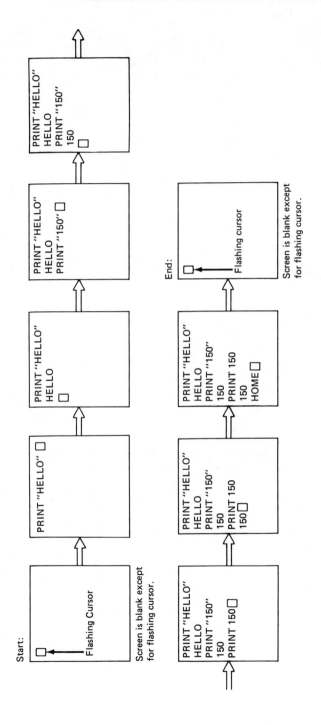

Figure 1.10 A sequence of frames representing commands entered in the immediate mode. (Note that the command HOME clears the screen.)

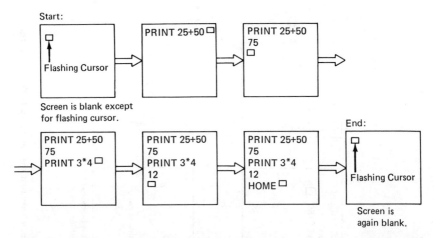

Figure 1.11 Another sequence of frames representing routine calculations. (Note that the asterisk symbol denotes multiplication; i.e., 2*2 yields 4.)

where n is one of the low-resolution "color numbers," given in Table 1.1. For example, the statement

$$COLOR = 15$$

would set the color to white. The color specification holds until the next "color" statement is entered. If no color specification is entered, the computer assumes a default value of zero, which is the

Table 1.1 Representative Set of Color Numbers for Low-Resolution Graphics.

Color Number	Color Name
0	Black
1	Magenta
2	Dark blue
3	Purple
4	Dark green
5	Gray
6	Medium blue
7	Light blue
8	Brown
9	Orange
10	Gray
11	Pink
12	Green
13	Yellow
14	Aqua
15	White

representation of black.   Since the screen is black to start with, graphic images illuminated in black do not show up.

To illuminate a rectangle in the specified color, enter a statement of the form:

PLOT x, y

where x represents the column number and y represents the row number.   This is roughly the same orientation as in coordinate geometry, except that the (0, 0) point is the upper left corner of the screen.   Thus, (0, 0) represents the upper left corner, (0, 39) represents the lower left corner, (39, 0) represents the upper right corner, and (39, 39) represents the lower right corner.   The immediate statement:

PLOT Ø,Ø

therefore, would light up the little rectangle in the upper left corner of the screen.[1]   Similarly, the statement

PLOT 39,Ø

would light up the upper right corner of the screen.   Figure 1.12 gives a sequence of frames that light up the four corners of the screen

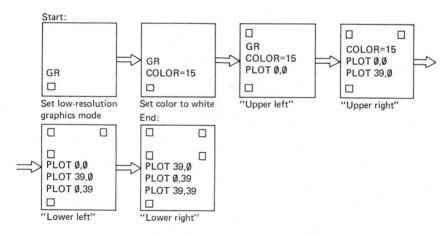

Figure 1.12   A sequence of frames representing graphics commands entered as immediate statements.

[1] Note that the zeros are slashed to distinguish them from the letter "oh." This is common practice with computers.

in white. The bottom four lines of the screen give the immediate commands, entered in the following sequence:

```
GR
COLOR=15
PLOT 0,0
PLOT 39,0
PLOT 0,39
PLOT 39,39
```

To return to the text mode from the low-resolution graphics mode, the user enters the TEXT command as follows:

```
TEXT
```

and then, as usual, presses the RETURN key.

Low-Resolution Lines

A line can be drawn on the screen by lighting up successive rectangles in either the vertical or the horizontal direction. For example, to draw an orange horizontal line from column 10 to column 15 in row 20, the following statements would be entered:

```
GR
COLOR=9
PLOT 10,20
PLOT 11,20
PLOT 12,20
PLOT 13,20
PLOT 14,20
PLOT 15,20
```

The result of the above script is depicted in Figure 1.13. The fundamental problem with this approach to drawing lines is practically obvious. In order to draw a line 40 rectangles in length, the execution of 40 statements would be necessary.

An easier way of drawing lines is to use the HLIN and VLIN statements, which stand for "horizontal" and "vertical" lines, respectively. A replication of the above horizontal line is specified as:

```
HLIN 10,15 AT 20
```

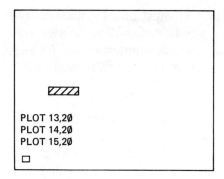

Figure 1.13   A line can be drawn by lighting up successive rectangles in either the horizontal or vertical direction.

which means: "Draw a horizontal line from column 10 to column 15 in the 20th row." In an analogous manner, the statement to draw a light blue vertical line from row 0 to row 39 in column 15 is specified as:

$$COLOR=7$$
$$VLIN\ 0,39\ AT\ 15$$

A frame showing the result of this VLIN statement is given in Figure 1.14.

High-Resolution Graphics Mode

High-resolution graphics statements are similar to low-resolution graphics statements except that an H, for high resolution, is placed

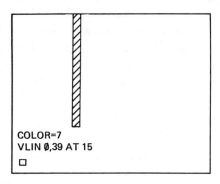

Figure 1.14   A frame depicting a vertical line drawn with the VLIN statement.

before most words. It must also be remembered that with high-resolution graphics, points, not small rectangles, are being lit up.

In order to place the computer in the high-resolution graphics mode, the user must type the HGR statement as follows:

HGR

and then press the RETURN key. When this command is received by the computer, the screen is cleared and the high-resolution graphics mode is entered. The bottom four lines of the screen are used for text, and the upper part of the screen is divided into a matrix of dots, which is 280 plotting points wide and 160 plotting points high. The points are numbered $\emptyset$ through 279 and $\emptyset$ through 159, respectively.

When a point is illuminated, two items of information are specified by the computer:

1. The color of the dot
2. The location of the dot

To set the color, enter a statement of the form:

HCOLOR=n

where n is one of the high-resolution color numbers, given in Table 1.2. The statement:

HCOLOR=2

for example, would set the color to violet. The color specification holds until the next H color statement is entered. If no color specification is entered, the computer assumes a default value of zero, which is the representation of black. As with low-resolution graphics, graphics images of black do not show up on a black background. One technique that can be used with black images is to give the background a color prior to presentation of the black image, if that is the intent of the viewer.

To illuminate a point in the specified color, enter a statement of the form:

HPLOT x,y

where x represents the column number and y represents the row number. This is the same representation as with low-resolution

Table 1.2 Representative Set of Color Numbers for High-Resolution Graphics.

Color Number	Color Name
0	Black 1
1	Green
2	Violet
3	White 1
4	Black 2
5	Orange
6	Blue
7	White 2

graphics, the (0, 0) point is the upper left corner of the screen. It follows that (0, 159) represents the lower left corner, (279, 0) represents the upper right corner, and (279, 159) represents the lower right corner of the screen. The immediate statement:

HPLOT 0,0

therefore, would light up the small dot in the upper left corner of the screen. Similarly, the statement

HPLOT 279,0

would light up the small dot in the upper right corner of the screen. The following script entered in the immediate mode:

HGR
HCOLOR=2
HPLOT 0,0
HPLOT 279,0
HPLOT 0,159
HPLOT 279, 159

would light up the four corner dots of the screen in violet. To return to the text mode from the high-resolution graphics mode, the TEXT command is entered, as with the low-resolution graphics mode.

High-Resolution Lines

A similar philosophy to that of low-resolution lines applies to high-resolution lines, except that it takes more points than rectangles to comprise a line so that the need for an automatic line drawing facility is even greater.

A convenient means of conceptualizing the screen in high-resolution graphics is to view it as a matrix of dots. Then to draw a line, it is necessary only to give the endpoints, as in the following example:

HPLOT 0,0 TO 279, 159

which draws a line from the upper left corner of the screen to the lower right corner of the screen. When drawing a high-resolution line, the computer takes care of the in-between points. Figure 1.15 shows a diagonal line drawn in the high-resolution graphics mode with the HPLOT statement.

There are several more options available with the HPLOT statement, but it will be necessary to do some programming in order to use them effectively.

GRAPHICS IN THE EXECUTION MODE

In order to do computer graphics in the execution mode, it is necessary to build a program that contains graphics statements. Then, when the program is executed with the RUN command, the intended visual image is created.

Suppose that it were desired to create in the color of orange the image given in Figure 1.16, which contains two lines and four rectangles created in the low-resolution graphics mode. A short program to create this frame is given as follows:

```
10 GR
20 COLOR=9
30 PLOT 0,0
40 PLOT 39,0
50 PLOT 39,39
60 PLOT 0,39
70 HLIN 0,39 AT 20
80 VLIN 0,39 AT 20
```

While the program is not complicated or elaborate in any way, it is rather obvious that a typing error is likely to occur when the program is entered. In the immediate mode, an error would require that the image be started from the beginning. In the program mode, an

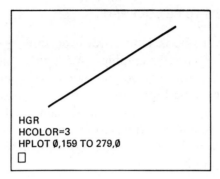

Figure 1.15 A frame depicting a diagonal line drawn in the high-resolution graphics mode with the HPLOT statement.

error causes no problem. To correct an error, all that need be done is to reenter the statement, since no visual image is created until the program is run. There are other advantages of using programs. A program can be saved on cassette tape or diskette and thereby preserved for distribution or future use. Also, a complicated program can be developed in stages if it can be saved between sessions on the computer.

Figure 1.17 gives a set of diagrams produced through the program given in Figure 1.18. This program uses high-resolution graphics and is probably a bit more complicated than the average person is accustomed to at this point. After the next several chapters, even this program will seem to be fairly simple.

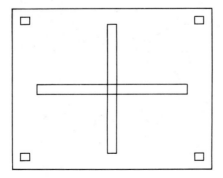

Figure 1.16 Low-resolution graphics image used to illustrate a graphics program (see text).

PREVIEW OF TOPICS TO BE COVERED

The objective of this book is to cover everything a person needs to know to do small-computer graphics. With this objective clearly in mind, a solid foundation in computer concepts and programming is necessary. After these topics are covered, the book continues with graphics technology; animation; two-dimensional images; three-dimensional images; and the translation, rotation, and projection of visual objects. Throughout the book, both low-resolution and high-resolution techniques are explained.

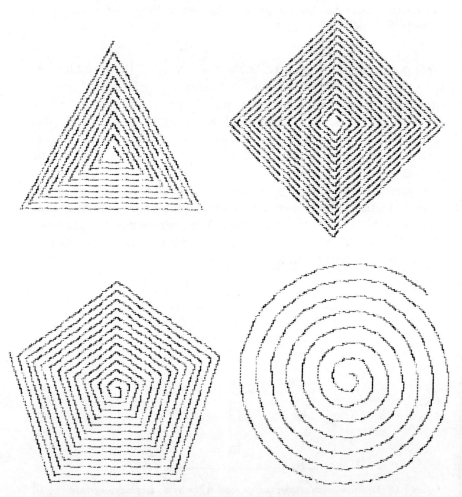

Figure 1.17 Collage of figures produced by the spiral program (see Figure 1.18).

```
JLIST

5   REM   HRES SPIRAL
6   HGR : HCOLOR= 3
10  PI = 3.14159
20  A1 = 0:A2 = 2 * PI
25  X0 = 140:Y0 = 80
30  INPUT "NUMBER OF SIDES ";N
40  INPUT "RADIUS OF POLYGON ";R
50  INPUT "INCREASE RADIUS BY ";F
60  D = (A2 - A1) / N
70  HPLOT X0 + R,Y0
80  FOR TH = A1 TO A2 + .01 STEP D
85  R = R + F: IF R > = 80 THEN 120
90  HPLOT  TO X0 + R *  COS (TH),Y0 + R *  SIN (TH)
100   NEXT TH
110   GOTO 30
120   END
```

Figure 1.18 High-resolution spiral program.

One of the most interesting applications of small-computer graphics involves business presentations, wherein graphs, histograms, and pie charts are used to summarize numerical data. Techniques of this type are presented after a thorough presentation of graphics technique is given.

VOCABULARY LIST

Knowledge of the following terms will aid the reader in becoming familiar with small-computer graphics:

Color device
Command mode
Disk unit
Display device
Execution mode
Frame
Graphics screen
Hardware
High-resolution graphics mode
Immediate statement
Input line

Keyboard unit
Low-resolution graphics mode
Microcomputer
Packaged program
Personal/home computer
Printer
Program
Program mode
Software
Tape cassette unit
Text mode

EXERCISES

1. The capability for generating color is a characteristic of _____ _____.

2. In order to do computer graphics, a person needs a _____ _____.

3. In a basic system, the _____ is used for data entry and output appears on the _____.

4. To do computer graphics, you need hardware and _____.

5. A _____ is an ordered collection of computer instructions.

6. The three screen modes are: _____, _____, _____.

7. Each text character position corresponds to how many low-resolution rectangles?

8. In high-resolution graphics, an image is generated as an arrangement of _____.

9. Which mode controls the operation of the computer?

10. Which mode is used to build programs?

11. Which mode is used to run programs?

12. Which statement puts the computer in the low-resolution graphics mode?

13. Which statement puts the computer in the high-resolution graphics mode?

14. What statement is used to set low-resolution color?

15. What statement is used to set high-resolution color?

16. What statements are used to draw low-resolution lines?

17. What statement is used to illuminate a low-resolution rectangle?

18. What statement is used to draw high-resolution lines?

19. What statement returns the computer from the graphics mode to the normal mode?

20. In the execution mode, the visual image is created when the program is ___ _____.

ANSWERS

1. The computer.
2. Computer, display device.
3. Keyboard, screen.
4. Software.
5. Program.
6. Text, low-resolution graphics, high-resolution graphics.
7. Two.
8. Dots.
9. Command.
10. Program.
11. Execution.
12. GR.
13. HGR.
14. COLOR.
15. HCOLOR.
16. HLIN and VLIN.
17. PLOT.
18. HPLOT.
19. TEXT.
20. Executed.

2
Applications and Programming Concepts

Small computers with graphics capability are designed to be used by persons with varying levels of computer knowledge. For some computer graphics applications, the computer can be programmed so that very little technical knowledge is required to actually operate the computer and apply it to a set of graphics needs. This category is the preprogrammed graphics software package mentioned in the first chapter. Operational knowledge of the computer is all that is required for this type of activity. Many persons, however, will want to program the computer themselves, because it is relatively easy to do, and because most modern small computers facilitate the programming process. Knowledge of programming methods and languages is needed for this type of activity. Lastly, the computer must be used productively in order to justify the financial investment in it. The recognition and specification of viable applications of computer graphics is known as graphics systems design, for which a basic knowledge of computer applications is needed. This book provides the three types of knowledge needed to successfully do computer graphics. The only prerequisite is an understanding of basic computer concepts, which is covered in this chapter.

MAJOR COMPUTER APPLICATIONS

One of the key factors in learning about computers is an understanding of the types of applications for which computers are used. Once the applications are recognized, then the key details about the structure of the computer and how to program it logically fall into place. The major applications of computers tend to parallel those for which human activity is inappropriate, inconvenient, or costly. Typical examples are extensive mathematical calculations, clerical operations, the retrieval of information, and the effective presentation of information — such as with computer graphics. In many applications, a computer is required because the typical person cannot respond quickly enough or be sufficiently accurate to satisfy operational constraints. In the following paragraphs, several general classes of computer applications are given. The classifications are more conceptual than actual, and a given computer application could possibly be placed in more than one class — depending upon whether the computer is used for scientific, business, administrative, or educational purposes.

Descriptive Computing

Descriptive computing, sometimes called problem solving, provides the user with more information on a subject, such as the design parameters of a bridge or road, the trajectory of a space vehicle, or the root of an equation. The subject under consideration is usually defined mathematically, and the formulas are used in the calculations.

Data Analysis

Data analysis is used to draw conclusions and make predictions from actual or experimental data. The associated techniques normally employ statistics and mathematics but frequently involve simple comparison and logical operations for checking tolerance conditions and determining combinations of events, respectively.

Data Processing

Data processing involves the storage, processing, and reporting of information. Although data processing is commonly associated with the accounting and record keeping functions of an organization, it is not generally restricted to business activity and may encompass a variety of clerical tasks, such as printing address labels, generating shipping orders, and scheduling work activities. The processing of survey and census data might also be placed in this category, as could be the computer preparation of an index for a book.

Modeling and Simulation

A *model* is an abstraction of a real-life situation from which we can draw conclusions or make predictions about the future; *simulation* is the use of models to attain the essence of a system without having to physically develop and test it. Through the use of computers, a realistic model of a system, such as the traffic flow in a city or the checkout procedure in a supermarket, can be developed and simulated to permit decision makers to evaluate alternatives in a reasonable time frame.

Optimization

The optimization class of computer application uses mathematical models to obtain the best solution to a given type of problem, for which a prototype solution has been developed. Typical applications are the calculation of the exact ingredients of sausage, the optimum assignment of personnel, and the most profitable allocation of capital investments.

Process Control

In process control, a computer is used in conjunction with a physical process or laboratory experiment to collect data or provide real-time control of the process. Through the use of sensory or control devices, the computer can communicate with a noncomputer device that is external to the computer system. The computer is programmed to sample the input signals on a periodic basis and compare the corresponding values against prescribed limits or store them for further study. When necessary, the computer can generate output signals to control a physical system, such as a temperature control system in a chemical plant. A common example of process control is the patient monitoring system in a hospital.

On-Line and Real-Time Systems

In an on-line or real-time system, the computer is connected via telecommunications facilities to a console device or to another computer system. Typical examples are the airline reservation system in most airports, savings bank systems used for checking balances and verifying credit, and the message switching systems used in the military. *On-line* means that communication is made directly with the computer, and *real-time* means that the computer is programmed to respond within a prescribed time period to satisfy the user's needs.

Information Systems

An information system is a collection of computer facilities, programs, and informational resources that permit the accumulation, classification, storage, and retrieval of large amounts of information. In some cases, an information system is designed and implemented as an on-line real-time system, and in other cases, it is not. Most information systems are designed to assign meaning to data — hence, the name information — in addition to storing data. Typical examples are inventory control systems, library information systems, insurance policy maintenance systems, and medical and legal information systems.

Education

One of the most rewarding applications of computers is in education, where the computer is used for administration, instruction, and problem solving. The administrative use of computers normally involves data processing and information systems and is used for record keeping, class scheduling, and curriculum planning. In instruction, the familiar technique of computer-assisted instruction (CAI) is used to enhance programmed learning. In problem solving, descriptive computing, data analysis, and optimization, methods are used to provide the student with problem-solving and analysis experience and to extend the range of problems that can be solved.

Computer Graphics

The visual presentation of information through the use of modern imaging techniques together with the power and flexibility of a modern computer provides a medium for both creativity and efficiency. As such, computer graphics is a distinct type of computer application and also an effective means of enhancing the other applications.

In general, any well-defined computational or retrieval procedure that can be broken down into a series of successive steps can be programmed for computer solution. However, computers cannot do everything. Computers have well-defined characteristics that make them useful for some applications and not for others. A computer can perform arithmetic and logical operations very quickly and with great accuracy and reliability. The computer can also be used to store larger amounts of information and can be programmed to make that information available at a moment's notice in either a textual or graphical form. Applications that require this type of service are generally enhanced through the use of the computer. On the other hand, applications that require inductive, intuitive, or adaptive behavior are not as well defined at this stage of modern technology and normally exist as research projects or laboratory experiments.

OVERVIEW OF INFORMATION PROCESSING

Similar to the manner in which humans must be taught to perform a task, the computer must also be taught to perform a computational procedure. The process of teaching the computer is known as programming. Because computers are machines, however, they possess no innate intelligence or free will and must be guided at each stage of a computation. The directions that are given to the computer are supplied by human beings. It necessarily follows that a person could perform the same calculations if enough time were available and the person were inclined to do them. In general, the basic functions performed during information processing are independent of whether they are executed by a computer or performed by a person. These functions are summarized in succeeding paragraphs.

Recording of Information

Information, or data in the language of the computer, can originate in several ways, such as the reading of a dial, the recording of an event in symbolic form, or the extraction of a value from a table, or as the result of a previous computation. The information can be recorded on paper in the form of prose, numerical data, or in graphical form, or it can be recorded on a computer-oriented medium such as punched cards or tape by a human operator. Information could also be recorded automatically on an electromechanical device, such as magnetic tape that is a part of a collection of laboratory experimental devices.

Transmittal of Information

Information is normally processed in a different location from that in which it is recorded. One of the primary advantages of many modern small computers is that they are portable, thereby extending the scope and convenience of computer applications. Traditionally, however, manual methods were used for transporting documents and records. Modern telecommunications facilities have reduced the need for manual methods and have provided the user with direct access to the information processing facility.

Information Storage

The storage of information is necessary before processing, during processing, and after processing. The form in which information is stored is to some extent dependent upon the processing involved but is also related to the processing device. For computer processing, information may be stored on the original recording medium, or it may pass through several stages of processing and eventually reside on a high-speed device suited to a particular application. For example, input data may be typed in at the keyboard of the computer, stored in the computer during processing, and then saved permanently on a diskette. The results of the processing may be presented to the user in the form of a printed report.

Information Processing

The specific characteristics of information processing depend upon the application. For science-based computations, a small amount of input data is followed by a relatively large number of mathematical calculations, which are followed by a small amount of computed results. For data processing computations, such as payroll or accounting, there is a large amount of input and output but a relatively small number of calculations. Most computer applications fall somewhere between the two extremes. In information retrieval, for example, very little processing is performed, and the primary function is to store and retrieve large amounts of information.

Information Reporting

Information resulting from the processing must ultimately be made available to the user in the form of a printed report, an updated file, the control of a physical process, a set of plotted points, a microfilm slide, or a graphics image.

In later sections, it will become evident that a computer is organized to perform the same functions, that is, input, processing, and output, along with a variety of supporting facilities for both data storage and graphic display. In applications of graphics, the processing may involve the translation, rotation, and projection of data so that the presentation of a particular visual image can be achieved.

DEVELOPMENT OF A COMPUTER APPLICATION

The popular thinking is that the development of a computer application is a very complex process and that special knowledge and training in computers is required to do the task successfully. Moreover, anyone who works with computers must certainly be a genius or, at least, close to one. For sure, computer people do not mind the reputation — even if it isn't true. As far as the complexity is concerned, development of a computer application is normally rather involved, but computer scientists have simplified the task considerably through the invention of easy-to-use programming languages. The BASIC language, covered in Chapter 1, is one of the best-known and most widely used languages of this type. Another important consideration is, of course, that development of a computer application is a typically human activity and, as such, can be broken down into well-defined steps that are easily performed.

Overview

The development of a computer application typically involves several people and a variety of different activities. The concept does not preclude a one-person operation but does recognize the fact that more than one person is usually involved. The steps in application development include the following types of activity and normally take place in the order given:

1. Problem definition
2. Systems analysis
3. Algorithm development
4. Programming
5. Debugging and testing
6. Documentation
7. Systems implementation

Each type of activity is discussed briefly.

Problem Definition

A potential problem requiring a computer solution manifests itself through a need of some kind. For example, a scientist may need to summarize his experimental data within a given time period or to a special degree of accuracy, or a businessman may need to resolve a paperwork problem that continually increases in scope and magnitude. A bowling alley proprietor may wish to streamline his bowling league operations, thereby attracting more leagues. A direct-mail firm may wish to computerize its mailing labels, replacing inefficient and outdated methods. The problem definition phase is characterized by the fact that the person recognizing the need is often limited in one or more of several ways:

1. He does not have the resources to solve the problem and must sell the new concept to higher management or administration.
2. He recognizes the need but is not sure of the best solution.
3. He is not sure that his needs can be satisfied with a computer.
4. He is not certain how a computer solution to his problem would fit into the total organization.
5. He is not confident of the validity of his need, is not sure that he can justify the solution, and prefers an outside opinion.

The best course of action to take in this case is to state the need precisely or formulate the problem exactly, as the originator sees it, and then call in a systems analyst from within the organization or an outside consultant to gather and analyze the facts relevant to the proposed application.

Systems Analysis

The process of analyzing a proposed computer application is performed by a person experienced in computer technology, applications, and organizational issues. More specifically, the systems analyst or consultant performs the following functions:

1. Determines whether the proposed application can be done
2. Develops the general methodology to be employed
3. Determines how the proposed computer application can be effectively integrated into the operational structure of the organization

If, during the performance of the above functions, it is determined that the proposed project is a viable one, then the systems analysis phase also includes a detailed flow analysis of the system or program and a specification of the inputs required and the outputs produced.

Algorithm Development

Algorithm development is the precise specification of the steps that comprise a computer program. In a data analysis application, for example, algorithm development would involve determining the statistical techniques and mathematical equations to be employed and the manner in which they would be used. In an inventory control application, algorithm development would involve the specification of methods for computing inventory levels, reorder points, and back-order requests. In a payroll application, algorithm development would be the identification of taxes and other deductions and the precise specification of the methods for computing gross and net pay. In a computer graphics application, algorithm development would involve the delineation of procedures using the graphics techniques necessary for producing the desired visual imagery. Algorithm development is not restricted to mathematical calculations and can involve any sort of computer procedure needed to produce the specified result.

Programming

Programming is the process of writing down the steps that comprise a computer program. If detailed program specifications were generated from the systems analysis and algorithm development phases, then computer programming would involve the straightforward coding of the program in a suitable programming language. If general specifications were produced during the systems analysis and algorithm development phases, then the programming phase would also involve the writing of detailed procedures in addition to coding. Computer programming is a detailed process that can easily result in a program that contains inadvertent errors. In fact, many programs contain errors that must be detected and removed.

Debugging and Testing

The process of running a program to determine if it contains errors is known as testing or program checkout, and the task of removing errors is known as debugging. Testing and debugging is achieved through the use of test cases that determine if the program operates correctly for each possible type of computation for which it was designed. Errors can occur in a variety of ways, including the following: incorrectly written program, faulty algorithm, poor systems analysis, and incorrect specification of applicable data values.

Documentation

The documentation phase includes the development of procedures for using the system or program and preparation of reports describing the procedures and internal structure of the program. Effective documentation is necessary when a person other than the original programmer is required to make changes in it.

Systems Implementation

Systems implementation is the process of putting the system or program into production. Some student, engineering, and scientific programs are developed and debugged, and computer results are obtained. Then the program is discarded. These are referred to as "one-shot" jobs. For these programs, documentation and implementation procedures are minimal. Other programs, such as those associated with information systems, data processing, and other commercial applications, may be used for years, going through change cycles to satisfy current needs. In the latter case, the effectiveness of a program should be monitored to ensure that the changing needs of the organization are satisfied.

COMPUTATIONAL PROCEDURES

Because a computer is a detailed and precise machine, the steps that comprise a computer procedure must be sufficiently detailed at each stage of a computation to permit the required calculations to be performed. Also, computer procedures do not solve one problem; they are designed to solve a whole class of similar problems. The procedure for adding two signed numbers a and b serves as an example:

1. If a and b have the same sign, go to step 5. (If a and b have different signs, continue with step 2.)
2. Subtract the smaller magnitude from the larger magnitude. (Continue with step 3.)
3. Give the result the sign of the number with the larger magnitude. (Continue with step 4.)
4. Stop.
5. Add the magnitudes of the numbers a and b. (Continue with step 6.)
6. Give the result the sign of number a. (Continue with step 7.)
7. Stop.

The procedure, even for this simple problem, is fairly detailed and would work for any two numbers a and b, for example, $(-5) + (-4) = -9$, $16 + (-11) = 5$, and $10 + 20 = 30$. A specific procedure of this type which exists as a finite list of instructions specifying a sequence of operations that gives the answer to any problem of a given type is called an *algorithm*. Computer programs are based on the concept of an algorithm.

Another familiar algorithm is used to generate a sequence of numbers known as Fibonacci numbers, which have amazing applications in the physical world. For example, Fibonacci numbers can be used to describe the arrangement of stems on a branch and the growth in a rabbit population. The Fibonacci sequence is depicted as follows:

$$1 \ 1 \ 2 \ 3 \ 4 \ 8 \ 13 \ 21 \ 34 \ \ldots$$

The pattern can be developed by inspection. After the first two numbers, each succeeding number is the sum of the previous two numbers. An algorithm for computing Fibonacci numbers that are less than 100 is given as follows:

1. Set N1 to 0. (This is not a Fibonacci number, and it is used only to start the process.)
2. Set N2 to 1. (This is the first Fibonacci number.)
3. Write down N2.
4. Set N3 equal to N1 + N2.
5. If N3 is greater than 100, then stop the calculations.
6. Write down N3.
7. Replace N1 by N2.
8. Replace N2 by N3.
9. Continue the calculations with step 4.

Clearly, an algorithm exists for each computational problem that has a general solution. The solution may exist as a set of mathematical equations that must be evaluated or as a set of procedural steps that satisfy a preestablished procedure — such as the well-known procedure for calculating income tax liability.

FLOWCHARTS

For many applications, a simple list of the steps that comprise an algorithm is sufficient for stating that algorithm in a clear and unambiguous manner. However, when the procedure is complex and different options exist, then a list of instructions is hard to follow. A typical example is a list of directions for locating a particular place in an unfamiliar city. When the directions are complex, a road map is preferred.

A flow diagram is used in the computer field for describing a complex process. A flow diagram — usually called a *flowchart* — may be comprised of symbols that represent the following functions:

Flow Direction. The flow of control is represented by an arrow. The arrowhead denotes the symbol to which control is passed.

Process. The rectangular process symbol denotes a computational operation.

Input/Output. An input or output operation is denoted by a parallelogram with slanted edges. Making information available for processing, that is, read in, is an input function. The recording or display, that is, read out, is an output function.

Decision. The diamond-shaped decision symbol is used to denote a change in direction of flow on a conditional basis.

Start-Stop. The terminal symbol denotes the beginning or end of a computational process.

Connection. The small circle serves as a connector between different points in a flowchart.

The flowcharting symbols are shown graphically in Figure 2.1.

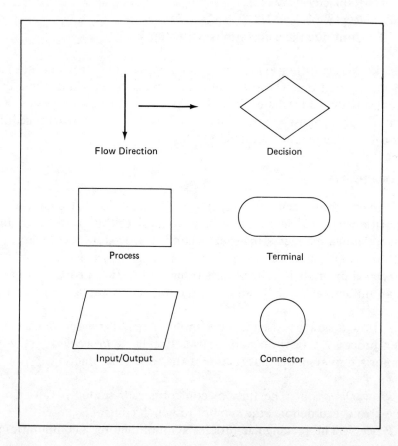

Figure 2.1 Flowcharting symbols.

A flowchart of the algorithm for generating Fibonacci numbers is given in Figure 2.2. One of the greatest benefits of the use of flow-charts is that the existence of repetitive operations can be detected at a glance. Figure 2.3 depicts another repetitive algorithm that computes the largest factor of an integer N. As in the previous examples, the flowchart gives a visual description of a procedure, and the type of operation performed at each stage of the computation is clearly evident by the flowcharting symbol used.

A computational procedure can also be described by the computer program used to perform the calculations. While a computer program has the same general characteristics as a list of instructions, the fact that meaningful statements that are computationally oriented can be used tends to reduce the complexity of this type of description. Using a program as a descriptive technique has the obvious advantage that if the program is correct, then the description of the algorithm is accurate.

COMPUTER PROGRAMS

A computer representation of an algorithmic process is a *computer program*. More specifically, a program is a meaningful sequence of statements in a special language designed for programming. Internal to the computer, a program is executed by a set of specific computer-oriented instructions that effectively controls the operation of the computer.

Statements in a Program

The statements in a program parallel the steps in an algorithmic process. Consider the problem of computing the largest factor of an integer N, given in Figure 2.3. The algorithm and the program in the BASIC language are listed as follows:

Algorithm	*BASIC Program*
1. Write down the number N.	1∅ INPUT N
2. Set M equal to the integer portion of $N/2$.	2∅ M=INT(N/2)

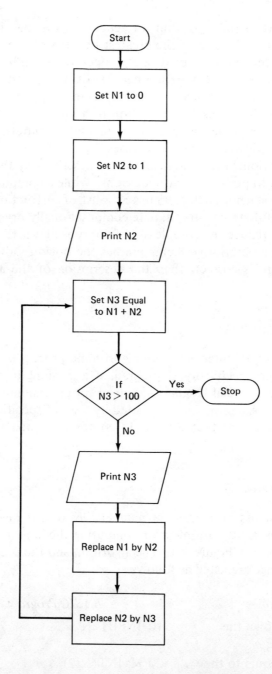

Figure 2.2   Flowchart of the algorithm for generating Fibonacci numbers.

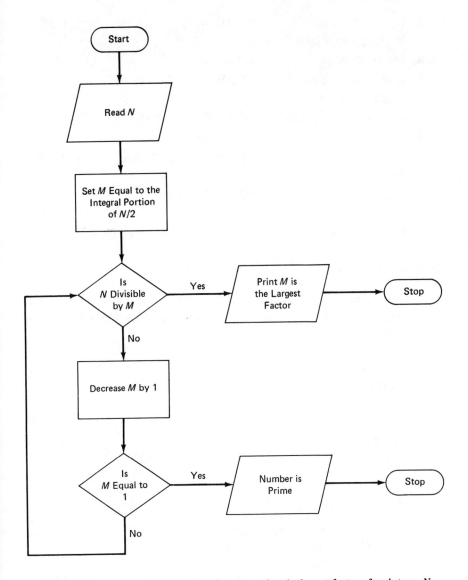

Figure 2.3 Flowchart of an algorithm for computing the largest factor of an integer N.

3. If N is divisible by M, go to step 8.	3Ø IF N/M=INT(N/M) GOTO 8Ø
4. Decrease M by 1.	4Ø M=M−1
5. If M is greater than 1, go to step 3.	5Ø IF M=1 GOTO 3Ø
6. Print number is prime.	6Ø PRINT N; " IS PRIME"
7. Stop.	7Ø STOP
8. Print "largest factor is" M.	8Ø PRINT "LARGEST FACTOR OF";
9. End algorithm.	9Ø END

A computer listing and execution of the program is given in Figure 2.4.

Structure of a Program

The structure of a program can be ascertained from the example. The program exists as a series of statements that perform three basic functions:

1. Input
2. Processing
3. Output

```
]LIST

10   INPUT N
20   M =  INT (N / 2)
30   IF N / M =  INT (N / M) THEN 80
40   M = M - 1
50   IF M > 1 THEN 30
60   PRINT N;" IS PRIME"
70   GOTO 90
80   PRINT "LARGEST FACTOR OF ";N;" IS ";M
90   END

]RUN
?477
LARGEST FACTOR OF 477 IS 159
```

Figure 2.4 Computer listing and execution of the largest-factor program.

In the example, the INPUT statement performs the input function, the PRINT statement performs the output function, and the IF, GOTO, and STOP statements perform the processing function. Lastly, the END statement denotes the end of the program.

VOCABULARY LIST

Knowledge of the following terms will aid the reader in becoming familiar with computer applications and programming:

Algorithm
Algorithm development
Computer graphics
Data analysis
Data processing
Debugging and testing
Descriptive computing
Documentation
Flowchart
Information processing
Information storage
Information system
Input
Modeling and simulation
On-line and real-time systems
Optimization
Output
Problem definition
Process control
Processing
Programming
Recording of information
Reporting
Systems analysis
Systems implementation
Transmission of information

EXERCISES

1. What class of computer application does the following:
   a. Provides more information on a subject.
   b. Draws conclusions from data.
   c. Involves the storage, processing, and reporting of information.

    d. Abstracts a real-life situation.

    e. Obtains the best solution to a problem.

    f. Communicates with a physical process.

    g. Connects the computer to a remote location.

    h. Permits retrieval of large amounts of information.

    i. Allows visual presentation of information.

2. Give the five steps in information processing.

3. List the seven steps in the development of a computer application.

4. What is a diagram of an algorithm called?

5. What is a finite list of instructions, describing a solution to a problem of a given type?

6. What are the three basic steps in a program?

ANSWERS

1. a. Descriptive computing.

    b. Data analysis.

    c. Data processing.

    d. Modeling.

    e. Optimization.

    f. Process control.

    g. On-line and real-time system.

    h. Information system.

    i. Computer graphics.

2. Recording, transmission, storage, processing, and reporting.

3. Problem definition, systems analysis, algorithm development, programming, debugging and testing, documentation, and systems implementation.

4. Flowchart.

5. Algorithm.

6. Input, processing, and output.

3
Introduction to Computers

Understanding computers is like understanding many aspects of the physical universe. On the surface an event or a physical entity may appear to be too complex to describe or understand. Once the event or entity is broken down into its component parts and basic laws or principles are applied, the complete system becomes understandable and is frequently manageable as well. The same kind of approach can be taken to understand computers and computer applications.

The following key point must be emphasized: *As in the case of the automobile and the airplane, a person need not be capable of designing and building a computer in order to realize and use its capabilities.* A working knowledge of the functional components of a computer is all that is needed to integrate a computer effectively as a component in an overall business or scientific information system or to utilize a computer in a problem-solving activity.

BASIC COMPUTER CONCEPTS

A computer can be conveniently viewed as an "information transformation machine," as depicted in Figure 3.1. The concept of computing is presented through the use of numbers because most people are familiar with them, so that the process of computing involves three "basic" steps:

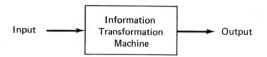

Figure 3.1 The computer can be viewed as an information transformation machine.

1. *Input,* whereby data on which the computer is to operate are entered into the machine
2. *Computing,* whereby the data are transformed to meet the needs of a given application
3. *Output,* whereby the results are made available for subsequent use

The notion of computing in this sense is certainly not new. For example, an ordinary mathematical operation, such as addition, uses a similar concept, shown as follows:

Input	Addition	Output
2, 3	operation	5

In general, the computer can be viewed as a "black-box" type of device that performs a well-defined operation on the input data and that produces appropriate output data.

If the computer is to be viewed as a black box, then it must be capable of operating automatically without human intervention — at least between elementary operations such as addition or division. This is, in fact, the precise manner in which it does operate, and this serves to distinguish an automatic computer from a calculator.

A USEFUL ANALOGY

As a means of introducing computers, it is useful to outline the steps people follow when solving a computational problem with the aid of a pencil and paper, desk calculator, slide rule, or ordinary adding machine. Human calculators usually have a list of instructions they are to follow and a set of input data. The process by which the calculations are performed can be summarized as follows:

1. *Information is stored* by writing the list of instructions, as well as input data, on the piece of paper. During the course of per-

forming the calculations, intermediate calculations are also written on the paper; however, people frequently keep some information in their heads while using charts and tables, and other information is held temporarily in the calculating device.

2. *Information is processed* by utilizing the computing device — that is, the slide rule, the desk calculator, or the adding machine — to perform the elementary calculations required by the computational process. Each operation is performed by taking data values from one place on the paper, performing the specified operation, and recording the result in a definite place elsewhere on the paper.

3. *The computational process is controlled* by referring to the list of instructions and by carrying each instruction out in a specified order. Each instruction is read, interpreted, and executed by the person performing the calculations, and the execution of an instruction is completed before the next is begun.

Although this is an oversimplified analogy to the functional structure of a computer, hardware components that correspond to the piece of paper and to human calculators and their computing devices actually exist; they are covered in the next section together with representative input, output, and mass storage devices.

COMPUTER SYSTEMS

The structure of a computer system parallels the three basic functions performed by a computer program: input, processing, and output. A set of hardware devices corresponds to each function, and this is the means by which the respective function is performed.

An overview diagram of a computer system is given in Figure 3.2. The major devices are:

1. The memory unit
2. The processing unit
3. Mass storage devices
4. Input devices
5. Output devices
6. A keyboard/display unit

The heart of a computer system is the processing unit and the memory unit, which effectively control the operation of the entire system and

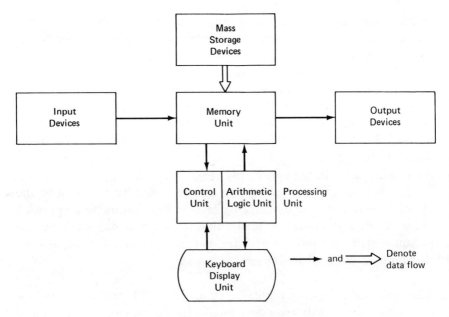

Figure 3.2   Overview of a computer system.

permit the system to operate automatically without human intervention. However, without the supporting devices in the system, the processing unit and the memory unit would be relatively ineffective.

The devices are presented in a general fashion, even though this book emphasizes computer graphics. This method of presentation will aid the reader in placing the concepts in proper perspective.

MEMORY UNIT

The memory unit is used to hold a program and its data during execution. The unit is synthesized from relatively expensive electronic components and is normally limited in size. Therefore, the memory unit is not used for the long-term storage of programs or data.

Before a program can be executed, it must be loaded into the memory unit. If the program resides on a mass storage device, such as a diskette, then it can be loaded with a keyboard command or with a statement from an executing program. A program may also be loaded into the memory unit from the keyboard on a statement-by-statement basis. Normally, when a program is entered into the computer for the first time, it is entered from the keyboard. It then can be saved on a mass storage device, so that it need not be entered again manually.

Data are handled in a manner similar to programs. Initially, data are entered from the keyboard. If small amounts of data are involved, then they are held in the memory unit during program execution and written to the mass storage device for long-term storage. If large amounts of data are used, then they are entered from the keyboard and written directly to the mass storage device because insufficient space would be available in the memory unit to hold all of the data. Subsequently, when an item of data is needed during the execution of a program, it can be read from the mass storage device.

It is wise to recognize that a program must be in the memory unit in order for it to be executed. However, only the data necessary to sustain the execution of a given statement must be in computer memory. Statements are available for transferring data between the memory unit and the mass storage device, so that careful program planning can extend the range of programs that can be executed.

The memory unit is volatile, which means that programs and data held there are lost when electrical power to the computer is turned off. Information to be saved must be placed on a mass storage device prior to termination of a computer session.

PROCESSING UNIT

The processing unit controls the operation of the entire computer system by fetching statements from the memory unit, interpreting them, and then executing the operations specified in the statements. The processing unit, or microprocessor as it is frequently called, is comprised of two components: a control unit and an arithmetic-logic unit. The control unit permits the computer to operate automatically, by going from one statement to the next without human intervention. (This is in contrast to the hand or desk calculator, which requires human interaction for each operation that is executed.) The control unit always keeps track of the location of the next statement in the memory unit. When the execution of the current statement has been completed by the arithmetic-logic unit, the control unit fetches the next instruction, interprets it, and passes control signals to the arithmetic-logic unit to have the required operations executed. The arithmetic-logic unit reads the needed data from the memory unit, performs the specified operations, and returns the computed result to the memory unit. When a nonarithmetic statement is to be executed, the operations are performed by either the control unit or the arithmetic-logic unit, depending upon the specific function required.

MASS STORAGE DEVICES

Mass storage devices are used to hold programs and data for long periods of time. Two main types of mass storage devices are in widespread use: sequential devices and direct-access devices. Sequential devices employ a serial medium such as magnetic tape. With a sequential device, the computer must pass over the $(i - 1)$st data element before the ith data element can be read. Direct-access devices use a rotating medium such as magnetic disk. Through the use of access arms, a data element can be located directly on a direct-access medium. Before a data item on a mass storage device can be used by the process unit, it must first be read into the memory unit. After being read into the memory unit, the original copy of the data item on the mass storage medium remains intact. The process of placing a data item on a mass storage device is regarded as an input function, and writing to a mass storage device is an output function. Mass storage devices are nonvolatile, which means that information stored on them is not lost when electrical power to the device is turned off.

Two types of mass storage devices are commonly available with small computers:

- Disk units
- Cassette tape units

A disk unit uses a diskette as a storage medium and provides direct-access storage capability. A cassette tape unit provides sequential storage capability and uses everyday cassette tape. Figure 3.3 gives a schematic of a diskette.

Figure 3.3 Diskette. (Courtesy Apple Computer Inc.)

INPUT AND OUTPUT DEVICES

In general, input and output devices include the following classes of equipment:

- Card readers and punches
- Paper tape readers and punches
- Printers
- Telecommunication terminals and consoles
- Special recognition equipment, such as badge readers, microfilm reader/writers, and check readers

Each type of device has a specific kind of recording medium and is used for a particular application. Most computers are designed to handle a wide variety of input and output devices. Collectively, input, output, and mass storage devices are known as *peripheral devices* because they are regarded as serving a peripheral role to the processing and memory units.

Some special input and output devices exist for small-computer graphics. One of the most popular input devices is a graphics tablet that digitizes an image as it is formed on the tablet. When an image is entered into the computer, it is stored in the memory unit for processing or for permanent storage on a diskette. Figure 3.4 shows a typical graphics tablet.

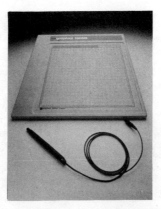

Figure 3.4 Graphics tablet. (Courtesy Apple Computer Inc.)

A popular output device is the graph plotter (Figure 3.5) that can draw curves under control of the processing unit. A graph plotter is one means of obtaining a hard-copy form of a graphics image.

Some printers for small computers provide the capability of displaying a "screen image" in hard-copy form. With a screen printer, any visual image projected on the screen can be transferred to the printing device. Figure 3.6 depicts a matrix printer of this type and an example of typical output in this class.

KEYBOARD AND DISPLAY UNITS

Input, output, and mass storage devices allow information to be transferred between an external device and the memory unit. The

Figure 3.5 HIPLOT DMP-4 six pen plotter. (Courtesy Bausch & Lomb)

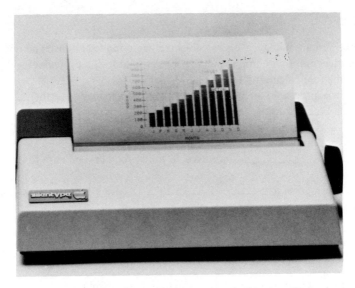

Figure 3.6 Matrix printer. (Courtesy Apple Computer Inc.)

keyboard and display units allow an operator to communicate directly with the processing unit and thereby control its operation.

For most graphics applications, all that is needed is the keyboard for input, the display screen for output, and a disk or tape unit for storage. When printed reports are required, then a printer can be used to obtain printed output.

VOCABULARY LIST

Knowledge of the following terms will aid the reader in becoming familiar with computers:

Arithmetic/logic unit	Magnetic disk
Black-box device	Mass storage device
Cassette tape unit	Memory unit
Control unit	Microprocessor
Direct-access device	Output device
Disk unit	Peripheral device
Input device	Processing unit
Keyboard/display unit	Sequential device

EXERCISES

1. In the human analogy, everyday objects correspond to computer components. Give the computer components that correspond to the following: (a) paper, (b) slide rule/calculator, (c) person.
2. Before a program can be executed, it must be loaded into the _____ _____ .
3. The _____ controls the operation of the entire computer system.
4. _____ are used to hold programs and data for long periods of time.
5. Cassette tape is a _____ device whereas magnetic disk is a _____ device.

ANSWERS

1. (a) Memory unit, (b) arithmetic/logic unit, (c) control unit.
2. Memory unit.
3. Processing unit.
4. Mass storage devices.
5. Sequential, direct-access.

4

Fundamentals of Programming

This chapter gives an overview of the fundamentals of programming and helps the reader ease into the BASIC language, covered in Chapter 5. This chapter also covers a few topics that are fundamental to computers, in general, to establish why various operational conventions exist.

LANGUAGE CONCEPTS

A *language* can be defined as a set of conventions used for communication. The conventions normally involve (1) the characters or letters, used for synthesizing language constructs, and (2) the rules that must be followed for developing the constructs in a meaningful way. Computer languages employ similar operating conventions.

Alphabet

The characters that can be used to construct statements are termed the *alphabet* of the language being used. Although there is much similarity between the alphabets of different computer languages, significant differences also exist.

Most programming languages use an alphabet that includes approximately 48 characters. The characters that comprise an alphabet are grouped into letters (A, B, and so forth), digits (1, 2, and so forth), and special characters (+, *, %, and so forth). The size of the alphabet has very little to do with the computer since a six-bit character permits 64 combinations (2^6) and an eight-bit byte permits 256 combinations (2^8). In many cases, however, the size of the alphabet is related to the number of printable characters on the card punch machine, the terminal device, or the line printer.

Statements

A program is a set of *statements* that serve to inform the computer of the processing to be performed. Statements are punched on cards or typed in at the computer terminal. Different statements must be separated in some way, and a convenient means of doing that is to start each statement on a new card or a new line. In many programming languages the end of a card (or line) denotes the end of a statement, unless a continuation is specified in some way, and a program is composed of a collection of data records (that is, cards or lines). In some programming languages a program is a string of characters formed by linking the data records that comprise the program. Each statement is terminated by a semicolon. Thus, a given line may contain one or more statements or parts of statements.

In subsequent chapters much of the discussion will concern statements and statement structure, and very little will be presented on the precise manner in which a statement is entered. This is because it is the statement itself that is of prime concern, and its means of representation is merely an operational convention.

DATA

In general, a computer program processes two types of data: numeric data and descriptive data. *Numeric data* would include items such as gross pay, the number of units of inventory, and a commission percentage. Thus, a numeric data item could be used in an arithmetic computation, such as when *hours* are multiplied by *rate* to obtain *gross pay. Descriptive data* would include items such as name, address, and age. Thus, a descriptive data item could *not* be used in an arithmetic computation.

Numeric Data

In ordinary arithmetic, calculations are performed on numbers represented as sequences of decimal digits, with possibly a decimal point and possibly an algebraic sign. A number of this type is called a *decimal number*. Thus, a decimal number x can be represented by an expression of the form:

$$x = n + 0.d_1 d_2 d_3 \ldots$$

where n is a signed or unsigned whole number and the d_is are digits in the range 0 through 9. The following constants are regarded as decimal numbers:

7	.00138
-19	-93000
+54.137	

Unneeded parts, such as the sign, decimal point, or fraction, need not be written — except as required by a particular application or programming language. A decimal number without a fraction is termed an *integer*.

Descriptive Data

A descriptive data item exists as a string of characters, and for that reason it is frequently referred to as *character data*. When a character constant is written in a computer program, the characters comprising the constant value are enclosed in quotation marks, such as:

$$\text{"INVENTORY ANALYSIS"}$$

A character constant, when written in a computer program, is frequently referred to as a *literal*. When character data is recorded on a storage medium — such as cards, tape, or disk — the quotation marks are not needed.

VARIABLES AND IDENTIFIERS

In mathematics the name given to an unknown quantity is *variable*. For example, one might say, "Let x equal the . . . ." In actual practice the concept is more general and enables principles to be developed independently of a particular problem.

Variables

The term *variable*, in contrast to the word *constant*, implies that a number can assume a set of values or, in other words, that the value of a variable is not constant but is subject to change. The equation:

$$y = 3x^2 + 2x + 5$$

for example, defines a second-degree polynomial for all real values of x. The letters x and y are variables.

A variable is also used as a symbolic name in everyday discourse. Thus, variables such as x or y are frequently used to represent an unknown quantity or to help in explaining a complex idea for which ordinary language is inadequate.

Identifiers

Symbolic names are frequently used in computing and are referred to as *identifiers,* because they identify something. In higher-level languages symbolic names are used for a variety of purposes — hence the more general name of identifier.

The most familiar type of identifier is used to name a data element that can change during the course of computation; it is termed a *variable*, as discussed above. Other identifiers are used to name statements and other entities. Sample identifiers are:

I

FOR

TO

Thus, in the BASIC statement:

FOR I = 1 TO N

The tokens FOR, I, TO, and N are identifiers and the number 1 is a constant. Of the four identifiers, FOR is a *statement identifier* that identifies a particular type of statement, I and N are variables, and TO is an identifier used as a *separator*, which is used to separate similar constructs such as two numbers in succession.

OPERATORS, EXPRESSIONS, AND REPLACEMENT

A computer can perform a variety of operational functions, known as *computing* or *computation*. Some of these functions are (1) arithmetic and logical operations, (2) data movement, (3) sequence and control functions, and (4) input and output. These operational functions are available to users through statements in a programming language, and when users desire to specify a particular type of operation, they pick the most appropriate statement for that purpose. Arithmetic and logical operations are particularly important. Assume that one desires to add the value of variable A to the value of variable B. This operation would be specified as:

$$A + B$$

This method is similar to ordinary mathematical notation and is the most frequently used method in programming.

Operators

In a programming language a symbol that denotes a computational operation is known as an operator. Thus, in the statement:

$$A + 1$$

for example, + is an operator; the variable A and the constant 1 are *operands* to the operator. If A has the value 7, then A+1 has the value 8. More specifically, an operand is a quantity upon which an operation is performed. An operand can be either a variable or a constant. Some operations, such as addition and subtraction, require two operands and are written with the operator symbol separating the operands. The expression A+B, to use an earlier example, denotes that the value of variable B should be added to the value of variable A. (The example is, of course, abbreviated since there is no indication of what to do with the result.) Other operators require a single operand, such as negation, and are written with the operator preceding the operand. The expression −A, for example, computes the expression 0−A and is used to change the sign of A. If A=10, then −A equals −10.

In computers, operators are classed into three general categories:

1. *Arithmetic operators* such as + (for addition and identity), – (for subtraction and negation), * (for multiplication), / (for division), and ** (for exponentiation)

2. *Comparison operators* that compare two data items (also referred to as relational operators), that is,

< for less than
≤ for less than or equal to
= for equal to
≥ for greater than or equal to
> for greater than
≠ for not equal to

3. *Logical operators* that determine the trust of one or more assertions, that is,

∧ for and
∨ for or
~ for not (or complement)

Table 4.1 gives informal definitions for the various operators.

Expressions

As in mathematics, operators and operands can be combined to form an expression denoting that a sequence of operations is to be performed. For example, A+B*C means that the product of B and C is to be added to A. Implied here is the fact that computational operations are executed in a prescribed sequence and that operators possess a priority that determines the order in which the operations are executed. A simple priority scheme is:

Priority	Operator
highest	**
↓	* or /
lowest	+ or –

which means that ** is executed before * or /, and so forth. Thus, the expression 2+3*4 has the value 14. Programmers can use the

Table 4.1 Operators.

Operation	Number of Operands	Form	Definition (R = result)	Example (↔denotes equivalence)
Arithmetic Operators				
Addition	2	$A + B$	$R = A + B$	$2 + 3 \leftrightarrow 5$
Subtraction	2	$A - B$	$R = A - B$	$6 - 4 \leftrightarrow 2$
Multiplication	2	$A * B$	$R = A \times B$	$4 * 3 \leftrightarrow 12$
Division	2	A/B	$R = A \div B$	$9/2 \leftrightarrow 4.5$
Exponentiation	2	$A ** B$	$R = A^B$	$3 ** 2 \leftrightarrow 9$
Negation	1	$-A$	$R = 0 - A$	$-A \leftrightarrow -3$, where $A = 3$
Identity	1	$+A$	$R = 0 + A$	$+A \leftrightarrow -5$, where $A = -5$
Logical Operators				
And	2	$Q \wedge T$	R is true if Q and T are both true and is false otherwise.	$T \wedge Q \leftrightarrow$ false
Or	2	$Q \vee T$	R is true if either Q or T is true and is false otherwise.	$T \wedge Q \leftrightarrow$ true
Not	1	$\sim Q$	R is true if Q is false; R is false if Q is true.	$\sim T \leftrightarrow$ false
Comparison Operators				
Less than	2	$A < B$	R is true if A is less than B and is false otherwise.	$3 < 2 \leftrightarrow$ false
Less than or equal to	2	$A \leqslant B$	R is true if A is less than or equal to B and is false otherwise.	$3 \leqslant 3 \leftrightarrow$ true
Equal to	2	$A = B$	R is true if A is equal to B and is false otherwise.	$3 = 2 \leftrightarrow$ false
Not equal to	2	$A \neq B$	R is true if A is not equal to B and is false otherwise.	$3 \neq 2 \leftrightarrow$ true
Greater than or equal to	2	$A \geqslant B$	R is true if A is greater than or equal to B and is false otherwise.	$2 \geqslant 3 \leftrightarrow$ false
Greater than	2	$A > B$	R is true if A is greater than B and is false otherwise.	$3 > 2 \leftrightarrow$ true

Note to logical operators examples: T=true and Q=false

priority of operators to their advantage. For example, the mathematical expression $ax^2 + b$ can be written in a programming language as A*X**2+B while maintaining the intended order of operations. In other cases, such as $\frac{(a+1)^2}{(a+b)}$, it is necessary to depart from the established order of execution. This need is served with parentheses that can be used for grouping. Expressions within parentheses are executed before the operations of which they are a part. The above example can be written in a programming language as (A+1)**2/(A+B). Similarly, the expression (2+3)*4 has the value 20. The use of parentheses can be extended to as many levels of nesting as are required by a particular sequence of operations.

Replacement and Data Movement

Expressions are permitted in some statements in a programming language because a computed value is frequently needed. For example, the following statement in the BASIC language:

IF A+B>13.5 GOTO 51∅

directs the flow of program control to the statement numbered 510 if the value of the expression A+B is greater than 13.5. However, the most frequent use of the expression is to specify that a set of computations are to be performed and that the value of a variable is to be replaced with the result. Thus, in the statement:

LET A=B+C

the value of A is replaced with the *value* of the expression B+C; this is called an *assignment statement.* The equals sign (=) denotes replacement but does imply equivalence since values and not expressions are involved. Thus if B contains the value 10 and C contains the value 20, then execution of the statement A=B+C causes A to be replaced with the value 30; B and C retain their original values.

In mathematics an identity such as:

$$(a+1)(a+2) = a^2 + 3a + 2$$

is commonly used. Statements of this type are strictly illegal in programming languages. The assignment takes the general form:

$$v = e$$

which means that the value of variable v is replaced with the value of the expression e, computed at the point of reference. The precise forms that v and e can assume are discussed later with respect to the different programming languages. In general, an expression e can be a constant, a variable, or a meaningful combination of constants, variables, operations, and parentheses. All of the following are valid expressions:

```
P          2**ML
25         (A1+B2) *C3-D4
I*J        A*B**2-1
DOG+CAT (A)
```

A simple assignment, such as:

NAME=C1

causes no computation to be performed and simply replaces NAME with the value C1, and C1 retains the original value.

ARRAYS

When a computer program deals with a large amount of data, such as the points in a graphics diagram, it is frequently cumbersome or literally impossible to assign each item a unique variable name. It is commonplace, therefore, to group items of data of the same type that are related to the same algorithmic process and give them a discriptive identifier. This kind of structure is called an *array*. Individual items are referenced by subscript, which gives their relative position in the array.

An example of array data could be the temperature on January 1 in various cities, given as follows:

Location	Temperature
New York	29°
Miami	69°
Chicago	26°
Los Angeles	60°
Minneapolis	15°
Seattle	35°

Clearly, the list could be very long, depending upon the purpose of the analysis. If this list were stored as an array, it would take the form given in Figure 4.1. To reference New York's temperature, an index of 1 would be used. To reference Los Angeles' temperature, an index of 4 would be used. When an array is referenced, the index is enclosed in parentheses following the array name. Thus $T(1)$ represents the New York value and $T(4)$ represents the Los Angeles value.

In some cases, an array is used to store a family of related data, such as the following "two-dimensional array" used to store temperature data for more than one date:

	TEMP	Date Index 1	2	3
	1	29	41	75
	2	69	79	92
Location	3	26	38	80
Index	4	60	67	88
	5	15	33	78
	6	35	41	73

It is important to recognize that only the array as a while need be given a name – in the latter case TEMP. The temperature in Miami, which has a location index of 2, on July 1, which has a date index of 3, is easily retrieved by writing TEMP (2, 3), and has a value of 92.

In computing, the concept of an array is extended to include n dimensions. The process of retrieving an element of an array, termed

Array T

Index	
1	29
2	69
3	26
4	60
5	15
6	35

Figure 4.1 An example of an array.

selection, uses the name of the array and the relative position of the desired element in the array. Indexes used to select an element from an array are termed a *subscript* and can be expressed as constants, variables, or expressions. The established practice is to reduce an index to an integer before selection takes place. The number of indexes in a subscript must equal the number of dimensions in the array. Thus, 'TEMP (3, 2),' in the above example, would select the value 38. When a subscript is written, the indexes are separated by commas and the entire set of indexes is enclosed in parentheses following the array name. The convention is used since subscripts or superscripts in the usual sense cannot be entered into the computer.

An array has several properties of interest. The array A, defined as:

$$a_{1,1} \; a_{1,2} \; a_{1,3}$$
$$a_{2,1} \; a_{2,2} \; a_{2,3}$$

can be used as an example. The first property is the *number of dimensions,* of which A has 2. Each dimension is further characterized by an *extent,* which is the number of array elements in a dimension. Another property is *homogeneity,* which refers to the fact that each element of an array must have the same data attribute. Thus, for example, an array must contain all numeric or all character values. Obviously, distinct values may differ.

VOCABULARY LIST

Knowledge of the following terms will aid the reader in becoming familiar with the fundamentals of programming:

Alphabet
Arithmetic operator
Array
Character data
Comparison operator
Computing
Data
Decimal data
Descriptive data
Expression
Homogeneity
Identifier

Index
Language
Logical operator
Numeric data
Operator
Replacement
Selection
Statement
Subscript
Variable

EXERCISES

1. A language normally uses a set of conventions that involve the _____ _____ and the _____ .
2. A program is a set of _____ .
3. The two basic forms of data are _____ and _____ _____ .
4. Character data is classed as _____ .
5. The name of a variable, statement, or separator is termed an _____ _____ .
6. Three types of operators are _____ , _____ _____ , and _____ .
7. The assignment statement does not denote equality but performs the _____ operation.
8. A group of related data selected by subscript is termed an _____ _____ .
9. The items in an array are _____ .
10. The number of subscripts in an array reference is equal to the _____ _____ .

ANSWERS

1. Alphabet, statements.
2. Statements.
3. Numeric, descriptive.
4. Descriptive data.
5. Identifier.
6. Arithmetic, comparison, logical.
7. Replacement.
8. Array.
9. Homogeneous.
10. Number of dimensions.

5

BASIC

The BASIC language achieves its greatest utility from the simple fact that it is easy to learn, easy to use, and easy to remember. (*BASIC* is an acronym for *B*eginner's *A*ll-purpose *S*ymbolic *I*nstruction *C*ode.) BASIC is particularly appropriate for the student or the data processing person who wants to utilize the advantages of computer processing without becoming a computer expert.

BASIC LANGUAGE STRUCTURE

BASIC was originally developed at Dartmouth College under the direction of Professors John G. Kemeny and Thomas E. Kurtz. BASIC has been under continuous development, and several implementations of the language are currently available at universities, through computer service companies, and in business concerns. Enhancements have been made to the original concept of BASIC, and one frequently hears of an "extended BASIC," "super BASIC," "advanced BASIC," and so forth; occasionally, one even hears of a "basic BASIC."

This chapter covers the original Dartmouth version of BASIC plus many of the subsequent extensions to the language. Variations exist between different implementations of the language. Any person making extensive use of the language should consult the reference manual for the system being used.

Fibonacci Numbers

As an example of the general appearance of a BASIC program, consider the Fibonacci sequence introduced earlier and depicted as follows:

$$1 \ 1 \ 2 \ 3 \ 5 \ 8 \ 13 \ 21 \ 34 \ \ldots$$

The pattern is clear; after the first two numbers, each succeeding number is the sum of the previous two numbers. A BASIC program that generates Fibonacci numbers less than or equal to 50 is given as follows:

```
]LIST

10   LET N1 = 0
20   LET N2 = 1
30   PRINT N2
40   LET N3 = N1 + N2
50   IF N3 > 50 THEN 99
60   PRINT N3
70   LET N1 = N2
80   LET N2 = N3
90   GOTO 40
99   END

]RUN
1
1
2
3
5
8
13
21
34
```

The above program is fairly obvious and will not be discussed further. After the next example, however, several statements, including those used above, will be described.

A Classic Problem

As an illustration of the manner in which BASIC can be used to solve a problem, consider this classic problem: Manhattan Island was sold by the Indians to the settlers in 1626 for $24 worth of beads and trinkets. At a given interest rate, what is the island worth today? A simple solution is presented in the following program:[1]

```
]LIST

10   LET P = 24
20   LET R = .06
30   FOR Y = 1627 TO 1982
40   LET P = P + P * R
50   NEXT Y
60   PRINT P
70   END

]RUN
2.44962315E+10
```

The statements numbered 10 and 20 assign the values 24 and 0.06 to the principal (P) and the interest rate (R), respectively. The interest for a given year is computed as P*R, and the principal at the end of a given year is computed as P+P*R. Statements 30 through 50 constitute a *program loop;* the principal is recomputed as the year (*Y*) advances from 1627 to 1982. After the loop is completed (that is, the number of iterations specified in statement 30 has been satisfied), the resulting principal (P) is printed in statement 60.

The PRINT statement can also be used to have several data items printed on the same output line by including those items in the PRINT statement, separated by commas or semicolons. Thus if statement 60 read,

60 PRINT "PRESENT VALUE OF MANHATTAN="; P

then the output would be,

PRESENT VALUE OF MANHATTAN=2.44962315E+10

---

[1] 2.44962315E+10 is the floating point form of 24,496,231,000.

Data items enclosed in quotation marks are printed as descriptive information, whereas the *numerical value* of an expression is printed. (Note that a variable, such as P, is an expression.)

In the preceding program, the data of the problem was built into the program (that is, a beginning principal of 24 and an interest rate of 0.06). If the user desired to repeat the calculations for different interest rates, then a set of data values would have to be established with a DATA statement, such as

$$\text{DATA } .\emptyset5, .\emptyset6, .\emptyset7, .\emptyset8$$

and the data set would have to be accessed with a READ statement, such as

$$\text{READ } R$$

Thus, a program to compute the present value of Manhattan Island for different interest rates is given as follows:

```
]LIST

10   DATA  .05,.06,.07,.08
20   FOR I = 1 TO 4
30   LET P = 24
40   READ R
50   FOR Y = 1627 TO 1982
60   LET P = P + P * R
70   NEXT Y
80   PRINT "PRESENT VALUE OF MANHATTAN=";P
90   NEXT I
99   END

]RUN
PRESENT VALUE OF MANHATTAN=838690475
PRESENT VALUE OF MANHATTAN=2.44962315E+10
PRESENT VALUE OF MANHATTAN=6.93164158E+11
PRESENT VALUE OF MANHATTAN=1.90137683E+13
```

The program includes a nested FOR loop that has the form:

$$A \begin{cases} \text{For} \ldots \\ \ldots \\ B \begin{cases} \text{For} \ldots \\ \ldots \\ \ldots \\ \text{NEXT} \ldots \end{cases} \\ \ldots \\ \text{NEXT} \ldots \end{cases}$$

The interpretation of the nested loops is as follows: For every iteration of loop A, loop B is executed from start to finish. Thus, if A is executed n times and loop B is executed m times, then a given statement contained in loop B is executed $n \times m$ times.

Several statements were used in the above examples:

LET — assigns the value of an expression to a variable

FOR — begins a program loop and specifies how many times it is executed

NEXT — ends a program loop and tells the computer to return to the beginning of the loop for the next iteration

PRINT — causes output data to be printed

DATA — creates a set of data

READ — causes data specified in a DATA statement to be accessed (read) and assigned to specified variables

END — ends a BASIC program

Each of these statements is described in more detail in later sections.

Characters and Symbols

A computer program is a coded form of an algorithm for solving a given problem on a computer. The statements of a program are encoded in the alphabet of the language using established conventions. It is necessary to distinguish between characters of the alphabet and symbols of the language. A *character of the alphabet* is an entity that has a representation internally and externally to the computer. The letter "A," for example, is a character of most language alphabets. The majority of characters have no meaning in their own right; for example, the letter "A" only has meaning through the manner in which it is used, which may be as part of a variable, the name of a statement, and so forth. Table 5.1 lists the BASIC alphabet, which consists of approximately 50 to 55 characters depending upon the equipment involved.

A *symbol of the language* is a series of one or more characters that has been assigned a specific meaning. Typical symbols are the plus

Table 5.1   Characters of the BASIC Alphabet.

Alphabetic Characters (26)
A B C D E F G H I J K L M N O P Q R S T U V W X Y Z
Digits (10)
0 1 2 3 4 5 6 7 8 9
Special Characters (19)

Name	Character
Blank	(no visual representation)
Equal sign	=
Plus sign	+
Minus sign	–
Asterisk	*
Solidus (slash)	/
Up arrow	↑
Left parenthesis	(
Right parenthesis	)
Comma	,
Point or period	.
Single quotation mark (apostrophe)	'
Double quotation mark	"
Semicolon	;
Question mark	?
"Less than" symbol	<
"Greater than" symbol	>
"Not equal" symbol	≠
Currency symbol (dollar sign)	$

sign (+) and the comma, used as a separator. A symbol consisting of more than one character is termed a *composite symbol,* and it is assigned a meaning not inherent in the constituent characters themselves. Typical composite symbols are ** for exponentiation and >= for "greater than or equal to." The symbols of the BASIC language are listed in Table 5.2.

In most implementations of BASIC, lowercase letters can be used interchangeably with uppercase letters. Spaces are ignored in BASIC, except with quotes, so that they can be inserted by the user to promote easy reading.

Data Types and Constant Values

Two types of data are permitted in BASIC, arithmetic data and character-string data. An *arithmetic data item* has a numeric value and is referenced through the use of a variable or a constant and

Table 5.2   Symbols of the BASIC language.

Symbol	Function	Alternate[a]
+	Addition or prefix +	
−	Subtraction or prefix −	
*	Multiplication	
/	Division	
↑	Exponentiation	∧
>	Greater than	GT
>=	Greater than or equal to	GE
=	Equal to (also see below)	
<>	Not equal to	≠ or NE
<	Less than	LT
<=	Less than or equal to	LE
;	Separates elements of list or subscripts	
.	Decimal point	
;	Separates elements of list	
=	Assignment symbol	
"	Used to enclose literals	
()	Enclose lists or group expressions	

[a]Some versions of BASIC use alternate composite symbols; frequently, the characters used are a function of the input devices available to the user.

may be generated as an intermediate result or as part of a computational procedure. BASIC accepts arithmetic constants in three principal forms:

1. As a constituent of a non-DATA statement, such as the number 5 in

LET A=B+5

2. As a constant in a DATA statement, such as

DATA 25, –13.289,.734E–4

3. In response to an input request (from an INPUT statement), such as

? – 75,4.56

In general, the arithmetic constant is written in the usual fashion, that is, as a sequence of digits possibly preceded by a plus or minus sign and possibly containing a decimal point. (An arithmetic constant is specified in decimal, and the user need not be concerned with how it is stored.) Sample arithmetic constants are –13.5, 12345, 1., +36, 0.01, –5, and 0. In addition, an arithmetic constant can be scaled by a power of 10 by following the constant with the letter E followed by the power, which must be expressed as either a positive or negative integer. Thus, the constant x E y is equivalent to the expression $x \times 10^y$ in mathematics. To cite some examples, .12E–4 is equivalent to 0.000012, –3E2 is equivalent to –300, +1.234E3 is equivalent to 1234, and –1E+1 is equivalent to –10. The sign of an arithmetic constant is frequently omitted in expressions by applying elementary rules of arithmetic. Thus, instead of writing A+(–5), most users simply write A–5. Similarly, A–(–5) would ordinarily be written as A+5.

In an arithmetic constant, the E (if used) must be preceded by at least one digit. Thus, 1E2 is a valid constant, whereas E2 is not.

A *character-string data item* is stored as a string of characters and can include any character recognized by the computer equipment. A character-string data item is referenced through the use of a variable or a constant. BASIC accepts character-string constants in three principal forms:

1. As a constituent part of a non-DATA statement, such as

    LET F$="TEA FOR TWO"

    or

    IF P$="END" THEN 1∅∅

2. As a constant in a DATA statement, such as

    DATA "BIG", "BAD"

3. In response to an input request (from an INPUT statement), such as

    ?"EACH HIS OWN"

A character-string constant must be enclosed in quotation marks. Any character within the quotes, including the blank character, is considered to be part of the character string. The length of a character string is the number of characters between the enclosing quotation marks. If quotation marks are to be included in the string, then the included mark must be represented as two consecutive quotation marks. The two consecutive quotation marks are a lexical feature of the language and are stored as a single character. Sample character-string constants are:

Character-String Constant	Length	Would Print As
"TEA FOR TWO"	11	TEA FOR TWO
"123.4"	5	123.4
" " "DARN IT" " "	9	"DARN IT"
"DON'T"	5	DON'T

Character-string data are frequently used for printing descriptive information, such as page and column headings, and are occasionally referred to in BASIC as *label data*.

Names

A *name* is a string of alphabetic or numeric characters, the first of which must be alphabetic. In BASIC, names are used to identify scalar variables, array variables, and functions.

A *scalar arithmetic variable* name (also referred to as a simple variable) consists of a single letter or a single letter followed by a single digit: A, I, Z1, and K9 are valid simple variables, while A10, DOG, and 3A are not. The initial value of a simple variable is zero, and it can only be used to represent arithmetic data.

A *scalar character-string variable* name (also referred to as a simple character variable) consists of a single letter followed by a dollar sign (that is, the currency symbol). The maximum length of a character string that can be assigned to a character-string variable is 18. The initial value of a simple character variable is 18 blanks. Thus, A$, I$, and S$ are valid simple character variables, while A1$, 5$, and IT$ are not.

Arrays

An *array* is a collection of data items of the same type (that is, all arithmetic data items or all character-string data items) that is referenced by a single array name. An *arithmetic array* can have either one or two dimensions and uses an identifier that consists of a single letter. An element of an array is referenced by giving the relative position of that element in the array. If the array has one dimension, then an element is referenced by appending a subscript enclosed in parentheses to the array name as follows:

$$a(e)$$

where a is the array name and e is an expression evaluated at the point of reference. Thus, the array reference $a(e)$ selects the eth element of array a. If the array has two dimensions, then an element is selected in a similar manner with an array reference of the form:

$$a(e_1, e_2)$$

where a is the array name and e_1 and e_2 are expressions evaluated at the point of reference. Thus, the array reference of $a(e_1, e_2)$ selects the element located in the e_1 th row and the e_2 th column of a. The following are valid array references: A(I), B(W4), C(P+1), C(I,J), E(T3/R+13, 3*X↑2-1), F(A(2*Q)), and G(B(1),4). The last two examples depict subscripted subscripts. All elements of an arithmetic array are initially set to zero when the program is executed.

A *character-string array* (referred to as a character array) can have one dimension and uses an identifier that consists of a letter followed by a dollar sign. Each element of a character array can contain up to 18 characters and is initially set to 18 blanks when the program is executed. As with an arithmetic array, an element of a character array is referenced by specifying the relative position of that element in the array with a construction of the form:

$$a\$(e)$$

where $a\$$ is the array name and e is an expression evaluated at the point of reference. The following are valid character array references:

B\$(3), C\$(2*J−1), and D\$(A(K)).

The extent of an array can be declared implicitly or explicitly. An *explicit array declaration* is made through the use of the dimension (DIM) statement, which is used to give the extent of each dimension of the array. Thus, the statement:

DIM P (3,4) Q (36) T\$ (17)

defines a two-dimensional arithmetic array P with three rows and four columns, a one-dimensional arithmetic array Q with 36 elements, and a character array T\$ with 17 elements, each element of which can contain a character string of 18 characters. The lower subscript bound for all array dimensions is one; the upper subscript bound is the value declared with the DIM statement. The DIM statement is presented in a later section on arrays.

An *implicit array declaration* is made when an array reference with either a single or a double subscript is made to an undeclared array. An array referenced in this way with a single subscript is assigned an extent of 10 with lower and upper subscript bounds of 1 and 10, respectively. An array referenced in this way with a double subscript is assigned row and column extents of 10; each dimension has lower and upper bounds of 1 and 10, respectively.

Operators and Expressions

Arithmetic and comparison operators are included as part of the BASIC language. Arithmetic operators are defined on arithmetic data and are classed as binary operators and unary operators. A *binary arithmetic operator* is used in the following manner:

$$\text{operand} \oplus \text{operand}$$

where an operand is defined as an arithmetic constant, a function reference, an element of an arithmetic array, or an expression enclosed in parentheses, and $\oplus$ is one of the following arithmetic operators: +, =, *, /, or ↑. A *unary arithmetic operator* is used in the following manner:

$$-\text{operand}$$

where "operand" has the same definition as given above. The use of a unary operator is restricted to the following cases:

1. As the leftmost character in an expression, provided that two operators do not appear in succession; or
2. As the leftmost character in a subexpression enclosed in parentheses such that the unary operator follows the left parenthesis.

An example of case 1 is –A+B↑C, while an example of case 2 is A*(-B↑(-3). The result of a binary or unary arithmetic operation is a numeric value.

An *arithmetic expression* can be an arithmetic scalar variable, an element of an arithmetic array, a numeric constant, a function reference, or a series of these constituents separated by binary operators and parentheses and possibly prefixed by unary operators. Thus, any of the following are valid expressions in BASIC:

A1	–(C1+I–1)	–SQR(X↑3)–J
B+25	SIN(X3)	((Y+3)*Y+16) *Y–1

As stated previously, parentheses are used for grouping, and expressions within expressions are executed before the operations of which they are a part. For example, the expression 2*(3+4) equals 14. When parentheses are not used in an arithmetic expression, an operand may appear as though it is an operand to two operators; that is, for example, the operand B in an expression such as:

$$A+B*C$$

In this case, operators are executed on a priority basis as governed by the following list:

Operator	Priority
↑ (that is, ∧)	Highest
unary −	
*, /	↓
binary +, binary −	Lowest

Thus, in the expression A+B*C the expression B*C is executed first, and the result of that subexpression is added to A. Operators of the same priority are executed in a left-to-right order.

A *character expression* is a character variable, a character array member, or a character constant. Except when they are used in a PRINT statement, character strings are handled in a special way:

1. If the character string contains less than 18 characters, it is padded on the right with blanks so that it can be stored as 18 characters.
2. If the character string contains more than 18 characters, it is truncated on the right so that its length is 18 characters.

(Character strings used in a PRINT statement are given a length determined by the enclosing quotation marks and the above conventions do not apply, that is, no padding or truncation occurs.)

A *comparison expression* has the form:

$$\text{operand} \oplus \text{operand}$$

where the "operands" can be either arithmetic expressions or character expressions (the operands cannot be mixed), and + is one of the following comparison operators: =, <>, >=, >, <=, or <. The result of a comparison expression is either a "true" value or a "false" value, which is used in the conditional IF statement. Thus, if A=10, B=15, C$="TEA", and D$="DOG", then the following valid comparison expressions give the indicated results:

A=B yields the value "false"[2]
A↑2+A*B>=B↑2 yields the value "true"
C$<>D$ yields the value "true"
(A+2.5)↑2>1∅1.5 yields the value "true"
C$<D$ yields the value "false"[3]

In an arithmetic comparison expression, the arithmetic expressions that serve as operands to the comparison operation are evaluated first; then the comparison operation is performed.

Statement Structure

BASIC is designed to be a language for time-sharing, and the structure of the language reflects that mode of operation. *Time-sharing* means that many users share the resources of the computer. Each statement in BASIC is prefixed with a *statement number* that serves two purposes:

1. BASIC statements are executed in an order determined by the arithmetic value of the statement number.
2. The statement number is used to reference another statement in statements such as

GOTO 5∅∅

In the first case, the statement number serves as a "line number," so that statements need not be entered in any specific order to facilitate the insertion, deletion, and modification of statements.

The form of a BASIC statement is:[4]

statement-number [statement-identifier] [statement-body]

where *statement-number* is an unsigned integer;[5] *statement-identifier* is a word that identifies a particular type of statement; and *statement-body* is a series of characters that comprise the body of the statement.

---

[2] Arithmetic comparisons use the arithmetic value of the operands.
[3] When BASIC (and as a matter of fact, any programming language) is implemented, an ordering sequence among characters is defined. Frequently, the ordering sequence is based on the numerical values of the internal representations of the characters.
[4] The syntactical conventions used to describe programming languages are covered in Appendix A.
[5] Usually, one to four decimal digits are permitted in a statement number.

Sample statements are:

$5\emptyset\emptyset$ LET A=B+C*D
$3\emptyset\emptyset$ LET K3=16
783   GOTO 1$\emptyset\emptyset$
91$\emptyset$ IF A>=B THEN 3$\emptyset\emptyset$
44$\emptyset$ STOP
999   END

Thus, a statement is constructed from a statement identifier, a statement body, or both. Neither a statement identifier nor a statement body is required, and thus a blank line (except for the statement number) is permitted to improve readability and to serve as a point of reference in a program. Blank lines are ignored by the computer.

A good programming practice is to insert comments to help a person remember what a particular set of statements does. A comment (that is, a remark) can be inserted anywhere in a program with a statement of the form:

statement-number REM[any character] . . .

For example, the following statements are comment lines:

35$\emptyset$ REM THIS PROGRAM IS INCORRECT
89$\emptyset$ REMARK FNG IS THE GAMMA FUNCTION

Comment lines are ignored by the computer.

Program Structure

A program in the BASIC language is characterized by the fact that a complete program must be entered before any part of the program is executed and by the fact that it is usually transparent to the user how the program is executed.

When the user has entered the complete program, a command is entered either to RUN the program or to LIST the program. After the computer has performed a requested action, it types a prompt character, such as], to inform the user that he or she can again enter either statements or commands.

The user can add or change a statement at any time by simply typing the statement number (of the line to be inserted or modified) followed by the new statement. When the program is run or listed, the statements are sorted by statement number, and new statements replace old ones. A statement is deleted by typing its statement number with a blank line.

Once the execution of a program is started, the program runs until a STOP statement is executed, an END statement is reached, a condition arises that prevents further execution, or the last statement in the program is reached. The following example depicts the preceding concepts:

```
]NEW

]100 DATA 3,4,5,12,7,24

]200 READ B,H

]300 LET D=SQR(B*B+H*H)

]400 PRINT B,H,D

]500 GOTO 200

]RUN
3               4               5
5              12              13
7              24              25

?OUT OF DATA ERROR IN 200
]150 PRINT "BASE","HEIGHT","DIAG"

]RUN
BASE           HEIGHT          DIAG
3               4               5
5              12              13
7              24              25

?OUT OF DATA ERROR IN 200
]LIST

100    DATA  3,4,5,12,7,24
150    PRINT "BASE","HEIGHT","DIAG"
200    READ B,H
300    LET D = SQR (B * B + H * H)
400    PRINT B,H,D
500    GOTO 200
```

Thus, the structure of a program in the BASIC language is inherent in the fact that it is a collection of statements ordered by a statement number (that is, line number).

INPUT AND OUTPUT STATEMENTS

This section and the following sections describe the various statements that comprise the core of the BASIC language. The statements are grouped by the functions they perform, and examples of the use of each type of statement are given.

Input and output statements are used to enter data into the computer and to display results to the user. Four statement types are presented: PRINT, DATA, READ, and INPUT.

PRINT Statement

The PRINT statement is used to display results on a person's output unit, which is usually a terminal device. The form of the PRINT statement is:

> PRINT expression [, | ; expression] . . .

where "expression" is an arithmetic or a character-string expression. The syntax of the PRINT statement denotes that the following cases are valid:

PRINT A	PRINT C, D1+3
PRINT 25	PRINT H; I
PRINT 2*B	PRINT J, K; L
PRINT A,B,C,D,E	PRINT "ABC"; M
PRINT	PRINT 2*A↑3+4*A+5

The key point is that expressions must be separated by a punctuation character that can either be a comma or a semicolon. Normally, the PRINT statement is used in a program as follows:

```
110 PRINT "3^2=",3^2

120 END

]RUN
3^2=          9
```

A comma is used as punctuation, and the output values are printed in columns. Each column has a width of 18 characters. When it is desired to run the fields together, a semicolon is used as a separator, as in the following example:

```
]10 PRINT "3^2=";3^2
]20 END

]RUN
3^2=9
```

When a PRINT statement is completed, the carriage is normally moved up to the next line. The user can prevent the carriage from advancing by ending the PRINT statement with either a comma or a semicolon. The following example illustrates the latter point:

```
]LIST

10   FOR I = 1 TO 5
20   PRINT I
30   NEXT I
40   END

]RUN
1
2
3
4
5
```

```
]LIST

10   FOR I = 1 TO 5
20   PRINT I;" ";
30   NEXT I
40   END

]RUN
1 2 3 4 5
```

A PRINT statement with no statement body simply advances the carriage line. Thus, in the following example:

```
110 PRINT "FIRST LINE"

120 PRINT

130 PRINT "NEXT LINE"

140 END

]RUN
FIRST LINE

NEXT LINE
```

a line on the printed page is skipped as a result of the "null" print statement (line 20).

DATA Statement

The DATA statement is used to create a data list internal to the computer, and has the form:

> DATA constant [, constant] . . .

where "constant" is an arithmetic or character constant. All data specified in DATA statements are collected into a single list; the order of the data constants is determined by the logical order of the DATA statements in the program. The internal data list can be accessed by the READ statement during the execution of a program. Actually, the DATA statement is a nonexecutable statement, and the internal data list is created before the program is executed. Thus, DATA statements can be placed anywhere in a program. The logical order of DATA statements is determined by the relative magnitude of associated statement numbers.

READ Statement

The READ statement is used to assign values to scalar and array variables and has the form:

> READ variable [, variable] . . .

where "variable" is an arithmetic or character scalar variable or a subscripted array variable. A pointer is associated with the internal data list constructed from the DATA statements in a program. Initially, this pointer is set to the first value in the data list. As READ statements are processed, successive values from the data list are assigned to the variables in the READ statements. Logically, the values in the data list are used up as READ statements are executed. Each value from the data list must be the same type as the variable to which it is assigned. Thus, it is the user's responsibility to ensure that data values are sequenced in the required order. If an attempt is made to "read" data when the data list is exhausted or when the type of a data value and the variable to which it is assigned do not agree, then a READ error results, and execution of the program is terminated. A READ error also occurs when an attempt is made to "read" data when no DATA statement exists in the program. Examples of the DATA and READ statements have been given previously. The following example depicts the use of character-string constants, as well as arithmetic constants:

```
]LIST

10   PRINT "GRADE REPORT"
20   PRINT
30   READ N$,T1,T2,T3
40   PRINT N$
50   PRINT "AVERAGE IS ";(T1 + T2 + T3) / 3
60   PRINT
70   GOTO 30
80   DATA  "R. ADAMS",80,90,76
90   DATA  "J. COTTON",50,71,68
100  DATA  "M. DODGER",100,86,96
110  END

]RUN
GRADE REPORT

R. ADAMS
AVERAGE IS 82
```

```
J. COTTON
AVERAGE IS 63

M. DODGER
AVERAGE IS 94


?OUT OF DATA ERROR IN 30
```

INPUT Statement

In some cases the data values to be used in a program are not known beforehand and must be entered by the user on a dynamic basis — that is, while the program is being executed. The INPUT statement allows the user to interact with an executing program and permits data values to be entered. The INPUT statement operates like the READ statement except that data is entered from the user's console instead of from an internal data set. The INPUT statement is placed in a program at the point at which the data is needed. The computer types a question mark (?), and the execution of the program is suspended until the required data is entered. Since a program can include several INPUT statements, most people precede the INPUT statement with a PRINT statement identifying the data that should be entered. The form of the INPUT statement is:

INPUT variable [, variable] . . .

where "variable" is an arithmetic or character scalar variable or a subscripted array variable. The following example depicts the use of the INPUT statement:

```
]LIST

10  PRINT "ENTER A,B"
20  INPUT A,B
30  PRINT "A+B=";A + B
40  PRINT "A*B=";A * B
50  GOTO 10
60  END
```

```
]RUN
ENTER A,B
?2,3
A+B=5
A*B=6
ENTER A,B
?3,4
A+B=7
A*B=12
ENTER A,B
```

The above program includes what is known as an *input loop;* in other words, program control is always directed to the statement numbered 10 and then to statement 20 (with the GOTO statement in line 50) to input new values for A and B. The user can terminate the loop by pressing the RESET key on the keyboard.

ASSIGNMENT STATEMENTS

The assignment statement permits a data value to be assigned to a scalar variable or to a subscripted array variable. Assignment statements include the simple LET statement and the conventional assignment statement.

Simple LET Statement

The LET statement has the form:

LET variable=expression

where "variable" is a scalar arithmetic variable or a subscripted arithmetic array variable, and "expression" is an arithmetic expression; or where "variable" is a scalar character-string variable or a subscripted character-string array variable, and "expression" is a character-string expression. The statement means: "Replace the value of the variable with the value of the expression evaluated at the point of reference in the program." The following examples depict valid LET statements:

```
LET A=10
LET BS="TEA FOR TWO"
LET C1=.00125*Z+3
```

LET D(14)=191.8
LET E$(I+1)="JOKER"
LET P(K,3*J+1)=A*B(L-2↑I

Conventional Assignment Statement

The use of the word LET in the assignment statement is a notational convenience and is not required in most implementations of BASIC. The form of the conventional assignment statement is:

variable=expression

where "variable" and "expression" are the same as defined above. Examples of valid assignment statements are:

A=1∅
B$="TEA FOR TWO"
P(K,3*J+1)=A*B(L-2)↑I

and so forth.

PROGRAM CONTROL

As was mentioned previously, statements in a program are executed sequentially until a statement is executed that alters the sequential flow of execution. Six statements are included in the BASIC language to control the manner in which a program is executed: GOTO, IF, END, STOP, FOR, and NEXT. The GOTO and IF statements are presented in this section and are used to alter the flow of program execution on an unconditional and on a conditional basis, respectively. The END and STOP statements are also covered briefly. The FOR and NEXT statements are used for looping and are described in the next section.

GOTO Statement

The GOTO statement has the form:

GOTO statement-number

where "statement-number" must be the line number associated with a statement in the program. If the statement number used as the operand to the GOTO statement does not exist in the program, then the condition is recognized and continued execution of the program is not permitted. Several examples of the GOTO statement have been given in previous sections.

IF Statement

The IF statement allows program control to be altered on a conditional basis, depending on the value of a "conditional" expression. The format of the IF statement is:

> IF comparison-expression THEN statement-number

If the "comparison-expression" has the value "true" (in other words, the condition holds), then program control passes to the statement whose statement number is specified. If the statement to which control is branched is a nonexecutable statement (such as a DATA statement), then program control is passed to the first executable statement following the specified nonexecutable statement. If the "comparison-expression" is "not true" (in other words, the condition does not hold), then the execution of the program continues with the first executable statement that logically follows the IF statement.

The following example, which computes the average of a list of values, depicts the use of a simple IF statement, as well as an assignment statement, a GOTO statement, and a remark statement. The list is terminated when the value –999 is reached.

Other examples of the IF statement are given in subsequent sections.

```
]LIST

10   READ V
20   IF V =  - 999 THEN 70
30   REM  S AND N ARE INITIALLY ZERO
40   S = S + V
50   N = N + 1
```

```
60   GOTO 10
70   PRINT "AVERAGE IS ";S / N
80   DATA  24,42,68,50,-999
90   END

]RUN
AVERAGE IS 46
```

END and STOP Statements

Every program written in the BASIC language must end with the END statement, which has the following format:

$$\boxed{\text{END}}$$

The END statement serves two purposes:

1. It denotes the logical end of the program, such that statements with statement numbers greater than that of the END statement are ignored by the computer.
2. It causes execution of a program to be terminated when program control flows to it.

The STOP statement, which takes the form:

$$\boxed{\text{STOP}}$$

causes execution of the program to be terminated. The STOP statement can be located anywhere in the program, making it unnecessary to branch to the END statement to terminate the execution of a program. Many algorithms require that a sequence of steps be repeated. An algorithm of this type is usually programmed in one of two ways: (1) The program steps are duplicated the required number of times; and (2) the program is written so that the same program steps are executed iteratively. The second method is preferred in complex programs or when the necessary number of iterations is not known beforehand.

LOOPING

Introduction to Iterative Procedures

A series of statements to be executed repetitively is termed a *loop;* the statements that comprise the loop are termed the *body of the loop;* and one pass through the loop is termed an *iteration.* The number of iterations is governed by a *control variable* that usually operates as follows:

1. The control variable is set to an *initial value.*
2. The value of the control variable is compared with a limit value. If the limit value is exceeded, then the loop is not executed, and the first executable statement following the body of the loop is executed.
3. The body of the loop is executed.
4. The value of the control variable is incremented by a specified value — frequently referred to as an *increment* or a *step.* (The implication is that the program "steps" through the loop as the control variable assumes a set of values.)
5. The value of the control variable is compared with a limit value. If the limit value is exceeded, then the loop is terminated, and program execution continues with the first executable statement following the body of the loop. Otherwise, execution of the loop continues with step 3.

The following BASIC program depicts a simple loop:

```
]LIST

5   REM  SUM OF EVEN INTEGERS <= N
10  PRINT "ENTER N";
20  INPUT N
30  S = 0
40  I = 2
50  IF I > N THEN 90
60  S = S + I
70  I = I + 2
```

```
80   IF I <  = N THEN 60
90   PRINT "SUM=";S
99   END

]RUN
ENTER N?11
SUM=30
```

The program depicts each of the above steps. The statement numbered 10 initializes the control variable I (step 1). The statement numbered 50 tests the control variable I against the limit N (step 2). Statement number 60 is the body of the loop (step 3). Statement number 70 increments the control variable (step 4) with a "step value" of 2. Statement number 80 tests the control variable against the limit (step 5); if the value of the control variable is less than or equal to the limit value, then program control is returned to the statement numbered 60 to repeat the loop.

Looping is such a frequently used technique in computer programming that special statements are defined to control the manner in which loops are executed.

FOR and NEXT Statements

Two statements are included in BASIC to facilitate the preparation of program loops. The FOR statement is used to start a loop; it specifies the control variable, its initial value, its limit value, and the step. The NEXT statement is used to close a loop; it specifies the control variable that should be "stepped." The previous loop written with the use of FOR and NEXT statements is given as follows:

```
]LIST

5    REM   SUM OF EVEN INTEGERS <= N
6    REM   USING THE FOR/NEXT STATEMENTS
10   PRINT "ENTER N";
20   INPUT N
30 S = 0
40   FOR I = 2 TO N STEP 2
50 S = S + I
```

```
60  NEXT I
70  PRINT "SUM=";S
99  END

]RUN
ENTER N?11
SUM=30
```

The statements between the FOR and the NEXT statements comprise the body of the loop.

The format of the FOR statement is given as:

FOR arithmetic-variable=arithmetic expression
TO arithmetic-expression [STEP arithmetic-expression]

where "arithmetic-variable" must be a scalar variable and "arithmetic-expression" must be a scalar expression. If the STEP clause is omitted, it is assumed to be +1. The format of the NEXT statement is:

NEXT arithmetic-variable

where "arithmetic-variable" is the same scalar variable that is used in the corresponding FOR statement.

The FOR and NEXT statements are used in pairs to delineate a FOR loop. The FOR statement establishes the control variable and specifies the initial value, limit value, and step value. (The three values are referred to as *control parameters.*) The NEXT statement tells the computer to perform the next iteration. The control parameters are evaluated when the FOR statement is executed and cannot be changed in the body of the loop. *However, the value of the control variable can be modified from within the body of the loop.* FOR loops can be nested — that is, there can be more than one loop — but they must not overlap each other.

Effective Use of FOR and NEXT Statements

It is important to recognize that the use of a FOR/NEXT loop is a means of achieving control in a computer program. It can be used in some cases to eliminate the need for the GOTO statement, as shown in the following program that computes *n* factorial:

```
]LIST

5   REM  FACTORIAL
10  FOR I = 1 TO 2 STEP 0
20  PRINT "ENTER N";
30  INPUT N
40 F = 1
50  FOR J = 2 TO N
60 F = F * J
70  NEXT J
80  PRINT N;" FACTORIAL IS ";F
90  NEXT I
99  END


]RUN
ENTER N?5
5 FACTORIAL IS 120
ENTER N?10
10 FACTORIAL IS 3628800
```

The above program depicts a nested loop (that is, a *double loop,* as it is frequently called). The outer loop is executed until the RESET key is pressed in response to the INPUT statement. The same effect could have been achieved with a FOR statement, such as:

$$FOR \ I=1 \ TO \ 10000$$

where the loop is not expected to execute for the full 10,000 iterations but will be terminated by a special condition, as shown. In a similar fashion, a FOR loop can be used to count the number of times a series of statements is executed; for example:

```
]LIST

5   REM  COUNT VALUES
10  DATA  8,10,7,20,15,0
20  FOR N = 1 TO 100
30  READ V
40  IF V = 0 THEN 70
50 S = S + V
60  NEXT N
70  PRINT "NUMBER OF VALUES=";N - 1
```

```
80  PRINT "AVERAGE =";S / (N - 1)
99  END

]RUN
NUMBER OF VALUES=5
AVERAGE =12
```

In addition, the FOR statement, as defined above, allows several useful options, three of which are:

1. There can be a nonintegral STEP.
2. There can be a negative STEP.
3. The value of the control variable can be changed in the FOR loop.

All three cases are shown in the following example:

```
]LIST

5   REM  NEGATIVE STEP
10  FOR D = 2 TO  - 2 STEP  - .5
20  IF D = 0 THEN 40
30  PRINT D,1 / D
40  NEXT D
99  END

]RUN
2                    .5
1.5                  .666666667
1                    1
.5                   2
-.5                  -2
-1                   -1
-1.5                 -.666666667
-2                   -.5
```

Other examples of the FOR loop are included in the next section, Arrays.

ARRAYS

Arrays are an important feature of most programming languages since a great many computer applications utilize the concept of a family of related data, referred to by a single name — the *array variable*. The subject of arrays is briefly considered in Chapter 9; this section goes into more detail on how arrays are defined and used. First, a very brief review: An *arithmetic array* can have either one or two dimensions; an arithmetic variable name must consist of a single letter. A *character array* must have one dimension only; its variable name must consist of a single letter followed by a dollar sign ($).

Implicitly Defined Arrays

An implicitly defined array is one that is used without being declared. A one-dimensional implicitly defined array has an extent of 10 with lower and upper subscript bounds of 1 and 10, respectively. A two-dimensional implicitly defined array has both row and column extents of 10; lower and upper subscript bounds for each dimension are also 1 and 10, respectively.

Implicitly defined arrays are allowed in BASIC for practical reasons:

1. "Small" arrays are frequently used, especially in an academic environment, and it is a convenience to be able to use an array of this type without having to define it. Also, not having to specify the size of a "small" array means that fewer characters have to be entered into the computer, and the chances of making a simple mistake are lessened.
2. Computer storage is sufficiently large to easily handle the storage requirements of implicitly defined arrays.
3. For large arrays, which *do* have to be declared, storage must be managed judiciously.

As an example of a case where the use of an implicitly defined array could be useful, consider the storage and retrieval of a parts list that takes the form:

Part Index	Part Name	Quantity	Unit Price
1	Place ZR41T	10	0.49
2	Hinge J33	5	1.26
3	0.5×3 Bolt	103	0.12
4	Washer 0.5 Alum	97	0.01
5	Nut 0.5 Hex	103	0.03
6	PT 4001 T	21	0.25

The program, which follows, first stores the "part name" as a string array and the "quantity" and "unit price" as a two-dimensional array. Then the user is allowed to input a part index, and the computer prints out the name, quantity, and the value of the inventory.

```
JLIST

5    REM   INVENTORY PROGRAM
6    REM   USES IMPLICITLY DEFINED ARRAYS
10   READ N
20   FOR J = 1 TO N
30   READ P$(J),D(J,1),D(J,2)
40   NEXT J
50   REM   RETRIEVE DATA
60   PRINT "ENTER PART INDEX"
70   INPUT I
80   IF I > N THEN 999
90   PRINT P$(I)
100  PRINT "QUANTITY=";D(I,1)
110  PRINT "UNIT PRICE=";D(I,2)
120  PRINT "TOTAL VALUE=$";D(I,1) * D(I,2)
130  PRINT
140  GOTO 60
200  DATA  6
210  DATA  "PART ZR41T",10,.49
220  DATA  "HINGE J33",5,1.26
230  DATA  ".5 X 3 BOLT",103,.12
240  DATA  "WASHER .5 ALUM",97,.01
250  DATA  "NUT .5 HEX",103,.03
260  DATA  PT 4001 Q",21,.25
999  END
```

```
]RUN
ENTER PART INDEX
?3
.5 X 3 BOLT
QUANTITY=103
UNIT PRICE=.12
TOTAL VALUE=$12.36

ENTER PART INDEX
?6
PT 4001 Q"
QUANTITY=21
UNIT PRICE=.25
TOTAL VALUE=$5.25

ENTER PART INDEX
?10
```

The values of the elements of an implicitly defined arithmetic array are set initially to zero, and the values of the elements of an implicitly defined character-string array are set initially to 18 blanks.

Explicitly Defined Arrays

An array is explicitly dimensioned with the DIM statement that has the following form:

DIM array-specification [, array-specification] . . .

where "array-specification" is defined as:

arithmetic-variable (integer-constant) [, integer-constant] . . .

or

character-variable (integer-constant)

where "integer-constant" must not be zero. The following example depicts valid array specifications:

DIM A(17), B$(54), C(15,25), D(3,2∅), E(1∅∅∅)

A one-dimensional array is specified as:

$$\text{DIM } a(n) \quad \text{or} \quad \text{DIM } a\$(n)$$

and has an extent of n with lower and upper subscript bounds of 1 and n, respectively. An element of a (or $a\$$) is selected by an array reference of the form $a(e)$ (or $a\$(E)$), where e is an arithmetic expression that is evaluated at the point of reference and truncated to an integer. Similarly, a two-dimensional array is specified as:

$$\text{DIM } a(m,n)$$

and has row and column extents of m and n, respectively. The lower and upper subscript bounds for the row extent and 1 and m, respectively, and the lower and upper subscript bounds for the column extent are 1 and n, respectively. An element of a is selected by an array reference of the form $a(e_1,e_2)$, where e_1 and e_2 are arithmetic expressions evaluated at the point of reference and truncated to integers.

The following example computes prime numbers using the Sieve of Eratosthenes (which is a means for finding prime numbers by writing down odd numbers from 3 up and by erasing the third number after 3, the fifth number after 5, the seventh number after 7, and so forth). The program requests a number N and then computes and prints the prime numbers less than or equal to N.

```
]LIST

5   REM  PRIME
10   DIM P(1000)
20   PRINT "ENTER N";
30   INPUT N
40   IF N > 1000 THEN 990
50   FOR I = 2 TO N
60   P(I) = I
70   NEXT I
80 L =  SQR (N)
90   FOR I = 2 TO L
100   IF P(I) = 0 THEN 140
110   FOR J = I + I TO N STEP I
120 P(J) = 0
130   NEXT J
140   NEXT I
150   PRINT
```

```
160   PRINT "PRIMES <";N
170   FOR I = 2 TO N
180   IF P(I) = 0 THEN 200
190   PRINT P(I);" ";
200   NEXT I
210   PRINT
220   GOTO 999
990   PRINT "TOO LARGE"
991   GOTO 20
999   END

]RUN
ENTER N?30

PRIMES <30
2 3 5 7 11 13 17 19 23 29
```

The program also depicts nested FOR loops and the variable control parameters that were mentioned in the preceding section.

As a final example of the use of one-dimensional arrays, the following program reads a list of numbers and sorts them in ascending order. The program utilizes an exchange technique, depicted as follows:

The program initially sets a flag (F) to zero. When an exchange is made, F is set to one. If both passes are made through the data without making an exchange, then the values are sorted and the program terminates. Otherwise, the process is repeated. The advantage of the exchange technique is that the process is efficient if the data is sorted or partially sorted beforehand.

```
]LIST

5   REM  ODD/EVEN EXCHANGE SORT
10   DIM W(100)
20   READ N
30   IF N > 100 THEN 990
40   FOR I = 1 TO N
50   READ W(I)
60   NEXT I
70 F = 0
80   FOR I = 1 TO N - 1 STEP 2
90   IF W(I) < = W(I + 1) THEN 140
100 T = W(I)
110 W(I) = W(I + 1)
120 W(I + 1) = T
130 F = 1
140   NEXT I
150   FOR I = 2 TO N - 1 STEP 2
160   IF W(I) < = W(I + 1) THEN 210
170 T = W(I)
180 W(I) = W(I + 1)
190 W(I + 1) = T
200 F = 1
210   NEXT I
220   IF F < > 0 THEN 70
230   PRINT "SORTED VALUES"
240   FOR I = 1 TO N
250   PRINT W(I);" ";
260   NEXT I
270   GOTO 999
280   DATA  12
```

```
290  DATA  3,-7,9,6,5,1,4,3,8,0,2,7
990  PRINT "TOO MANY VALUES"
991  GOTO 20
999  END

jRUN
SORTED VALUES
-7 0 1 2 3 3 4 5 6 7 8 9
```

Two-dimensional arrays are defined and used in a similar manner, and the student is directed to the readings for more information on this subject. One of the features of the full BASIC language is a set of matrix input/output statements that permit a complete array to be read or printed with one BASIC statement.

FUNCTIONS

The computer is frequently used in applications that require the use of a mathematical function, such as the sine, cosine, or square root. In the computer, functions such as these are usually approximated to a given degree of accuracy with an algorithm such as the following series expansion for the trigonometric sine:

$$\sin x = x - \frac{x^3}{3!} + \frac{x^5}{5!} - \frac{x^7}{7!} + \ldots$$

Two options exist:

1. Users can program their own mathematical functions.
2. A set of frequently used functions can be provided as part of the programming language.

Usually, the second option is selected since not all users are versed in computer approximations, and it is convenient not to have to bother with them. Moreover, approximations can be coded efficiently in assembler language and placed in a program library to be shared by all users.

Built-in Functions

Functions that are supplied as part of the programming languages are referred to as *built-in functions*. The form of a function reference is the function name followed by an arithmetic expression in parentheses. The expression is evaluated at the point of reference, and the specified function is applied to the value of the expression. The function returns a value that can be used as an operand in the expression. Thus, the expression 2+SQR(25) has the value 7, where SQR is the square root function.

The *function name* for a built-in function is comprised of three letters that have a mnemonic relationship to the function they name. The form of a function reference is:

function-name (arithmetic-expression)

where "function-name" is one of the mathematical functions defined in the implementation of the language. Table 5.3 lists the built-in functions included in the original Dartmouth version of BASIC. All of the functions listed in Table 5.3 operate on a single value.

The following list gives some mathematical expressions that include functions and their equivalent representation in BASIC:

Mathematical Expression	*BASIC Expression*
$1 - \sin^2 x$	SQR(1-SIN(X)↑2)
$\cos 30°$	COS (3∅*(3.14159/18∅)) or COS (3.14159/6)
$a^2 + b^2 - 2ab \cos c_1$	SQR(A↑2+B↑2-2*A*B*COS(C1))
$\tan^{-1}(x/y)$	ATN(X/Y)
$\dfrac{e^x - e^{-x}}{2}$	(EXP(X)-EXP(-X))/2
$(|x|)2↑3$	ABS(X)↑3

When a function reference is used as an operand, as in SIN(X)↑2 or ABS(X)↑3, the function is applied first, and the result of the function is used in the arithmetic operation. In other words, a function reference has a higher priority than any of the arithmetic operators.

Table 5.3 Built-in Functions.

Function Reference	Definition
SIN (x)	Computes the sine of x radians.
COS (x)	Computes the cosine of x radians.
TAN (x)	Computes the tangent of x radians.
ATN (x)	Computes the arctangent in radians of the argument x; the result is in the range $-90°$ to $+90°$.
EXP (x)	Computes the value of e raised to the x power; that is, e^x.
LOG (x)	Computes the natural logarithm (that is, ln $|x|$) of the absolute value of x.
ABS (x)	Computes the absolute value of x (that is, $|x|$).
SQR (x)	Computes the square root of x, where $x \geqslant 0$.
INT (x)	Computes the largest integer $\leqslant x$.
SGN (x)	Returns the sign of x; if $x<0$, then SGN$(x)=-1$; if $x=0$, then SGN $(x)=0$; and if $x>0$, then SGN $(x)=+1$.

Internal Constants

An *internal constant* is a frequently used arithmetic value that is defined in the BASIC language. Three internal constants that are often used are pi, *e*, and the square root of 2, listed as follows:

Identifier	*Approximate Value (short form)*
&PI	3.14159
&E	2.71828
&SQR2	1.41421

Internal constants eliminate the need to remember and enter frequently used arithmetic values. An internal constant is treated as an ordinary operand.

VOCABULARY LIST

Knowledge of the following terms will aid the reader in learning the BASIC language:

Arithmetic data item
Arithmetic expression

Array
Binary operator
Body of the loop
Built-in function
Character
Character expression
Composite symbol
Control variable
DATA
DIM
END
Explicit array declaration
FOR
GOTO
IF
Implicit array declaration
Increment
Initial value
INPUT
Internal constant
Iteration
LET
Limit value
Loop
Name
NEXT
PRINT
Quotation marks
READ
Scalar
Statement
Statement number
Step
STOP
Symbol
Unary operator

EXERCISES

1. Study the program to determine the present value of Manhattan given in the chapter. Why is it necessary to include the following program loop?

FOR Y=1627 TO 1982
LET P=P+P*R
NEXT Y

2. Distinguish between a "character" and a "symbol."
3. With regard to the use of exponential notation for writing constants, the following statement can be made: "In an arithmetic constant, the E (if used) must be preceded by at least one digit." Why?
4. What function does the dollar sign ($) serve for naming character-string data items?
5. How do you delete a statement in a BASIC program?
6. How do you replace a statement in a BASIC program?
7. In what order are the statements that comprise a BASIC program executed?
8. Which of the following expressions are valid?

A+-B	(((34)))	Ø$+1
+/A	A$<63	T$(3)
A(B(2))	-E+F	X(-4)
D(E+1)	W(-1)	X+Y-1>13.4

9. What is an "implicit array declaration"?
10. Give an example of a character constant.
11. Give errors (if any) in the following BASIC statements:
    a. LET AB=16
    b. LET A3=K+1Ø,ØØØ
    c. LET F$='DON'T"
    d. REED A,B,C
    e. DATA 4E-3
    f. LET A=W+3.12.3
    g. LET K13=-3E-1
12. Discuss the execution of the following program segment using the material given in the chapter:
    LET A=3
    LET B=6
    LET C=B/A+C
    PRINT D
13. Write a BASIC program to compute the product of the numbers 2E3, 173.89, -14.839, 63.1, and .123E-1 and to print the result.
14. A depositor puts $10 per month in the bank. Interest is 6% per year compounded monthly. Write a BASIC program to compute the amount the depositor has in the account after 20 years.
15. Write a BASIC program that compute N! (that is, N factorial) and operates as follows: The computer requests that the user enter a number (N). After

verifying that the number is a positive integer, the computer computes N°, prints it, and then requests another number. Error diagnostics should be printed if the number is not a positive integer.

16. Write a BASIC program to compute the sum of the numbers less than 100 that are divisible by 7.

17. Given a set of numbers of the form:

$$\text{DATA } n, x^1, x^2, \ldots x^n$$

(allow for at least 100 values) write a BASIC program that computes and prints the following:
   a. Sum of numbers in the list and average value
   b. Largest number
   c. Smallest number
   d. Number of numbers equal to 20
   e. Number of numbers greater than 50 and less than 75

ANSWERS

1. It is necessary because the program computes the interest for each year (P*R), adds it to the principal (P+P*R), and then replaces the old principal with the new principal (P=P+P*R). It does this for *each* year in the given interval.

2. A *character* is simply a token from the character set. A *symbol* has a meaning in its own right, such as the plus (+) sign.

3. Because if E is not preceded by a digit,

$$E4 \quad \text{or} \quad E+1$$

for example, would be valid expressions.

4. It distinguishes a character variable from a numeric variable.

5. Enter the statement number with a blank line.

6. Enter a new statement with the same statement number.

7. The statements are ordered by statement number and executed accordingly.

8. The invalid statements are:

Statement	Reason
$\emptyset\$+1$	type mismatch
$+/A$	two operators in succession
$A\$<63$	type mismatch
$X(-4)$	illegal subscript
$W(-1)$	illegal subscript

The others are OK.

9. It is an array that does not have to be declared.

10. "TEA FOR TWO".

11. a. AB is an illegal variable in most forms of BASIC. However, some versions permit it.

 b. 10,000 is an illegal constant because of the comma.

 c. The character constant 'DON'T' is illegal. It should be written "DON'T".

 d. REED is an illegal statement identifier.

 e. The statement is correct.

 f. The constant 3.12.3 has an extra decimal point.

 g. The statement is correct.

12. The values of variables are initially zero. Therefore, after the first three statements are executed, we have the following:

$$\text{A contains 3}$$
$$\text{B contains 6}$$
$$\text{C contains 2}$$
$$\text{D contains } \emptyset$$

Then $\emptyset$ is printed.

13.
```
]LIST

10 P = 1
20 FOR I = 1 TO 5
30 READ A
40 P = P * A
50 NEXT I
60 PRINT P
70 DATA 2E3,173.89,-14.839,63.1,.123E-1

]RUN
-4005379.85
```

14.
```
]LIST

10 P = 0
20 R = .06 / 12
30 FOR M = 1 TO 240
40 P = P + P * R + 10
50 NEXT M
60 P = INT (P * 100) / 100
70 PRINT "$";P;" IS IN THE ACCOUNT"
```

15.

```
]LIST

10 S = 0
20  FOR I = 1 TO 100
30  IF  INT (I / 7) <  > I / 7 THEN 50
40 S = S + I
50  NEXT I
60  PRINT "SUM=";S

]RUN
SUM=735
```

16.

```
]LIST

10  PRINT "ENTER NUMBER - ZERO TO END"
20  INPUT N
30  IF  INT (N) = N THEN 60
40  PRINT "NOT POSITIVE INTEGER"
50  GOTO 10
60  IF N < 0 THEN 40
70  IF N = 0 THEN 999
80 P = 1
90  FOR I = 1 TO N
100 P = P * I
110  NEXT I
120  PRINT N;" FACTORIAL = ";P
130  GOTO 10
999  END

]RUN
ENTER NUMBER - ZERO TO END
?7
7 FACTORIAL = 5040
ENTER NUMBER - ZERO TO END
?0
```

17.

```
JLIST

5   REM   VARIABLES:
6   REM      S=SUM, S1=SMALLEST, L=LARGEST
7   REM      C1 = EQUAL TO 20
8   REM      C2 = GT 50 AND LT 75
10  DIM X(100)
20  READ N
30  FOR I = 1 TO N
40  READ X(I)
50  NEXT I
60  S = 0:C1 = 0:C2 = 0
70  S1 = X(1):L = X(1)
80  FOR I = 1 TO N
90  S = S + X(I)
100 IF X(I) >  = S1 THEN 120
110 S1 = X(I)
120 IF X(I) <  = L THEN 140
130 L = X(I)
140 IF X(I) <  > 20 THEN 160
150 C1 = C1 + 1
160 IF (X(I) <  = 50) OR (X(I) >  = 75) THEN 175
170 C2 = C2 + 1
175 NEXT I
180 PRINT "SUM=";S
190 PRINT "AVERAGE=";S / N
200 PRINT "SMALLEST=";S1
210 PRINT "LARGEST=";L
220 PRINT "# EQUAL TO 20=";C1
230 PRINT "# GT 50 AND LT 75=";C2
240 PRINT "END OF REPORT"
250 DATA  5
260 DATA  60,70,20,30,80

JRUN
SUM=260
AVERAGE=52
SMALLEST=20
LARGEST=80
# EQUAL TO 20=1
# GT 50 AND LT 75=2
END OF REPORT
```

6

Graphics Technology:
A Nontechnical Introduction

Modern graphics technology has come a long way since the early days of computers. There was a time when graphics facilities existed only in the domain of organizations with medium- to large-scale computers. It is rather obvious from the preceding chapters that the situation has changed somewhat in recent years, so that most organizations and many people can own a small computer with graphics capability. The big change was brought about by two aspects of technology:

- The availability of inexpensive microcomputers
- Advances in electronic display technology

Clearly, the computer part has already been covered. Electronic display technology has evolved from pen plotters to raster-scan techniques. In between, vector graphics and various forms of micrographics image generation were experienced. Most forms of graphic output (and input as well) are still in use today. However, a small window of this technology is currently available to the everyday user, at a reasonable cost and with relative ease of use. This chapter is primarily oriented to the needs of the small-computer user with graphics interests.

OVERVIEW OF A GRAPHICS SYSTEM

A graphic system has a general structure, independent of its cost and electronic sophistication. A schematic of a hypothetical graphics system is given in Figure 6.1. In sophisticated graphic systems re-quiring a high level of computing power, each component would normally exist as a separate box. In small systems, several components may be integrated into the same cabinet or share a common set of circuit boards. The various components are summarized in the following paragraphs.

Computer

The computer drives the graphics system by generating a video image through whatever forms of input, processing, and output are required. One of the primary components of the computer, per se, from the standpoint of small-computer graphics, is the memory used to store images. In most small-computer graphics systems, the memory is referred to as RAM, which is an acronym for random-access memory. Some programs that are used by the video circuitry are stored in a special read-only memory (ROM). Programs stored in ROM may not be changed by the user. Most nontechnical persons consider ROM programs to be part of the computer circuitry.

Mass Storage

Mass storage is used for storing programs, input data, and graphics images. With small computers, the mass storage is usually diskette or tape cassette. In other computers, mass storage is usually hard disk or conventional computer magnetic tape.

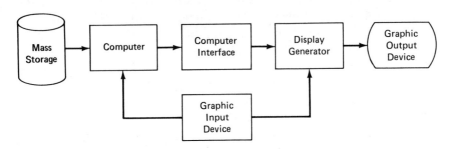

Figure 6.1   Schematic of a graphics system.

Computer Interface

The interface can be an electronic device or a storage medium. In early systems, the interface took the form of a magnetic tape that was physically transported to a pen plotter. In sophisticated electronic systems, the interface takes the form of a set of analog-to-digital and digital-to-analog conventions. In small computers, an electronic video display circuit is used.

Display Generator

The display generator produces information in a form for graphic display. The generator may be integrated into the computer interface or the display device, or be a stand-alone component. In general, the display generator is comprised of four systems: display controller, display processor, refresh memory, and video driver.

Graphic Device

The graphic device in a modern video graphics system is a screen-oriented device, although in older systems it took the form of a pen plotter in many cases. Most modern devices are either TV oriented or cathode-ray tube (CRT) oriented. The TV-oriented devices produce images by scanning and can be an ordinary home television set or a video monitor device such as those in a TV station. The CRT-oriented devices produce images by electron-gun deflection.

Graphic Input Device

A graphic input device takes one of three general forms: a tablet, a light pen, or a scanner. When an image is presented to an input device, it is transferred to the computer and to the video generator. A *graphics tablet* permits a user to literally draw an image on a small flat tablet with a transmitting device that looks like a pen. The image is digitized and entered into the video system. The image also goes to the screen so that the person can tell what he or she is drawing. This type of device, which serves as a drawing board, is popular among artists, designers, planners, and other persons who require a visual orientation for their work. A *light pen* is used in conjunction with a special CRT-output device to communicate with the computer by interrupting a program that drives the video unit at a designated position. The position at which a video display is interrupted can then be used by a computer program to process the relevant input. A *scanner* is a special optical device that digitizes an image prior to input. Image data that has been entered into the computer by optical means can then be processed by the computer as though it were entered through a manual procedure.

Image Processing of Graphic Input

Regardless of the method of entry, image data can be stored, processed, regenerated for output in another form, or simply viewed for its esthetic value. In some research and development applications, image processing can take the form of a sophisticated algorithm to recognize a pattern or identify a particular object. In some technical applications, image processing can take the form of procedures for "straightening lines" or completing complex figures. In many applications of image processing, figures can simply be moved to obtain different orientations or to create a desired visual effect. The essence of the situation is that images can be generated by the computer through instructions entered by the user, or be entered into the computer via some kind of graphic input device.

IMAGE TECHNOLOGY – VECTOR-STROKE GRAPHICS VERSUS RASTER-SCAN GRAPHICS

The differences in image technology are based upon the way that the graphics output device forms an image. The two most widely used methods are vector-stroke graphics and raster-scan graphics. Other technologies are available, but they will be mentioned only briefly.

Vector-Stroke Graphics

Vector-stroke graphics is an older method of generating images through the use of a cathode-ray tube (CRT) device and a collection of analog circuitry. In vector-stroke graphics, a beam of electrons can be moved to an arbitrary (x,y) position on the screen. Because the beam can be moved anywhere on the screen, this method is commonly referred to as *random-position technique*. In using vector-stroke devices, the deflection to the established (x,y) point can be made with the "beam on" or the "beam off." When the beam is off, a point at (x,y) is generated. When the beam is on, a line (or vector) from the current (x,y) position to the new (x,y) position is generated — hence the name vector-stroke graphics. When using vector-stroke graphics, the computer sends (x,y) points to the CRT, along with appropriate control information, through the digital-to-analog converter (see Figure 6.2). Thus, the vector-stroke graphics device functions as an ordinary computer output device. A typical vector-stroke graphics device is that when a vector from (x_1,y_1) to (x_2,y_2) is drawn, an actual straight line appears on the screen.

Raster-Scan Graphics

Raster-scan displays are useful for applications where high resolution is not required, either for technical or for economic reasons. The raster-scan technology uses a left-to-right scanning method — as in ordinary home television. Since the device must constantly be refreshed, as with television, a refresh memory is required to store an image, as suggested by Figure 6.3. In high-cost raster-scan systems, the various components may be integrated into the display device itself or in a stand-alone interface unit.

In small computers, the computer's memory serves as the needed refresh memory, and the video device exists in the TV set or in an equivalent display monitor (Figure 6.4). Normally, an area in RAM is set aside for the "graphics buffer," and the video output driver uses it to refresh the TV set or video monitor. Whenever it is desired to change the image being displayed, all a program need do is modify the graphics buffer. The PLOT, HPLOT, HLIN, and VLIN commands, covered in Chapter 1, just literally change the contents of the buffer.

Because of the widespread availability of TV sets, the raster-scanning method is particularly appropriate for low-cost computer

Figure 6.2 Vector-stroke graphics.

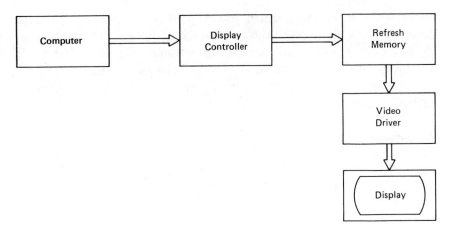

Figure 6.3   Raster-scan technology.

systems. A typical raster-scan graphics device has a resolution of
512×512 points. Most small-computer systems produce only a resolution of 200×300 points, and as a result, many lines do not appear
on the screen as "straight" lines. This topic is covered further in
Chapter 8, High-Resolution Graphics.

Raster Scanning

Raster scanning is the process used in TV sets and display monitors
with raster-scan graphics whereby an image is generated by deflecting
the beam in a horizontal pattern across the screen. American television
uses 525 lines per frame, and up to 1024 points can be defined per
line. (A *frame* can be regarded as a total visual image – such as one
"instant" on a TV set.) To preserve a continuous image without

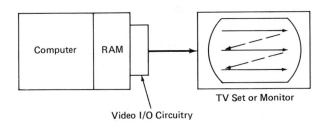

Figure 6.4   Raster-scan graphics for small computers.

flicker, the screen is scanned during two successive cycles called *fields*. One field produces the odd-numbered lines and the other produces the even-numbered lines. Thus, a frame consists of two fields produced during two scanning cycles. Television bandwidth limits the scanning rate to 30 frames per second. The process of scanning alternate lines is known as *interlacing*.

Other Technologies

In addition to beam-directed CRT devices and raster-scanning devices, other display technologies include the following:

- Direct-view storage tubes
- Flat (AC or DC plasma panels)
- Liquid crystal displays

Hobbs and Machover, et al.[1] give excellent overviews of modern graphics technology.

REFRESH MEMORY

Inherent in the preceding sections is the simple fact that the processing capability of a small personal computer cannot keep up with the continuous refresh time requirements of a modern TV set or video monitor. Thus, a graphics buffer is used to drive the video display. This buffer serves as a refresh memory, so that all that the video circuitry need do to refresh the screen is to access the memory, while the microprocessor is free to do other processing.

Bit Mapping

The primary method used to store video data in RAM is to let one bit in RAM correspond to a point on the screen. Thus, a 280×192 high-resolution display would require 53,760 bits or 6720 eight-bit bytes. Each screen dot, represented by a bit in memory, is called a *pixel,* for picture element.

When an HPLOT statement is entered as a command or in the BASIC language, it causes one or more bits to be set in refresh mem-

---

[1] See bibliographical references 1, 2, and 3 at the end of this chapter.

ory. Then the refresh circuitry takes over and the "new" image is generated.

Character Generation

Characters are composed of dots so that an 8×7-dot character (see Chapter 1) would require 56 bits using bit mapping, so a 40×40-character display would need 8960 bits or 1120 bytes of RAM for video refresh. Modern computer technology, commonly used in programming and data processing, permits a character to be stored in six to eight bits depending upon the internal coding system. Assuming an eight-bit byte is used to store one character, the 160-character screen, for example, would require only 160 bytes of RAM.

A character generator is built into the circuitry of the computer to convert an eight-bit character to the 8×7-dot matrix required for bit mapping. The character generation technique is used for both the text and the low-resolution graphics modes, and significantly reduces the amount of refresh memory needed for these modes of operation.

Graphics Modes

The preceding discussion of bit mapping and character generation explains to some extent the low-resolution, high-resolution, and text modes of operation. Not only are different areas of RAM used for refresh memory, but also, different video circuitry for image generation is employed.

SPECIAL BIBLIOGRAPHY ON GRAPHICS TECHNOLOGY

In spite of the widespread popularity of small-computer graphics, there are surprisingly few references to the technology of graphic display and image generation. The following bibliographical items are particularly well written and serve as a good starting place for in-depth knowledge of the subject matter.

1. Hobbs, L. C., "Computer graphics display hardware," *IEEE Computer Graphics and Applications,* Volume 1, Number 1 (January, 1981), pp. 25–39.
2. Machover, C., Neighbors, M., and Stuart, C., "Graphics displays," *IEEE Spectrum* (August, 1977), pp. 24–32.

3. Machover, C., Neighbors, M., and Stuart, C., "Graphics displays: factors in systems design," *IEEE Spectrum* (October, 1977), pp. 23-27.
4. Watson, A., "A simplified theory of video graphics, Part 1," *Byte* (November, 1980), pp. 180-189.
5. Watson, A., "A simplified theory of video graphics, Part 2," *Byte* (December, 1980), pp. 142-156.

VOCABULARY LIST

Knowledge of the following terms will aid the reader in becoming familiar with graphics technology:

Bit mapping
Character generation
Computer interface
Display generation
Field
Frame
Graphic device
Graphic input device
Graphics tablet
Interlacing
Light pen
Pixel
Raster-scan graphics
Refresh memory
Scanner
Vector-stroke graphics

EXERCISES

1. Name two factors that led to the widespread popularity of small-computer graphics.
2. What component drives a graphics system?
3. What component is used to store programs, data, and images?
4. Modern graphics devices are _____ .
5. During raster scan, the image is held in _____ .
6. Graphics input takes three forms. Name them.
7. Which graphics technology gives better resolution, vector-stroke graphics or raster-scan graphics?

8. Graphics commands cause the contents of what device to be updated?
9. High-resolution graphics uses _____ . Low-resolution graphics and the text mode use _____ .
10. A picture element is called a _____ .

ANSWERS

1. Microcomputers and raster-scan techniques.
2. Computer.
3. Mass storage.
4. Screen oriented.
5. Refresh memory.
6. Graphics tablet, light pen, and scanner.
7. Vector-stroke graphics.
8. RAM (refresh memory).
9. Bit mapping, character generation.
10. Pixel.

7

Low-Resolution Graphics

The subjects of low-resolution and high-resolution graphics were introduced in earlier chapters. This chapter gives some of the techniques that apply to low-resolution graphics. High-resolution techniques are covered in Chapter 8. Low-resolution graphics can take several convenient forms. Because of its simplicity, low-resolution graphics lends itself to easy programming and a variety of interesting applications.

TEXT GRAPHICS

Most of us have seen pictures of people and objects generated by a computer printer. Shading is achieved by selecting appropriate characters so that an image takes on a respectable resemblance to the object portrayed. This section gives the basic technology of how it is done and demonstrates the concepts through an interesting example. Text graphics has been used for many years to display data in the form of mathematical curves and histograms, to generate artistic figures, and to draw computer-generated schematics for business and industry.

Basic Technique

When text graphics is done, the image is stored as a two-dimensional array of characters, such as would be defined by the following declaration in the BASIC language:

$$DIM\ L\$(2\emptyset,4\emptyset)$$

This array would store an image that is 20×40 characters. The basic idea is to create an image through the following sequence of steps:

1. Fill the array with a background character, such as the blank (or space) character.
2. Place non-background characters in the array at appropriate places to create an image.
3. Print or display the array to achieve the desired effect.

Clearly, the major advantage of text graphics is that no special computer graphics equipment is needed — just a computer and a printer.

Illustrative Example — Game of Life

An interesting illustrative example of text graphics is the game of life, which simulates the increase and decrease of a population based on a simple set of rules. The game can be visualized on a rectangular grid, such as that given in Figure 7.1. Each cell in the grid has eight neighboring cells, as shown in Figure 7.2.

The grid is assigned an initial set of tokens, as shown in Figure 7.3, and the simulation proceeds according to the following rules as the population evolves:

- A cell survives to the next generation if it has two or three neighbors.
- A cell dies if it has four or more neighbors (overpopulation) or one or fewer neighbors (loneliness).
- A birth is made in an empty cell if it has exactly three neighbors.

All births and deaths occur simultaneously as the simulation passes from one generation to the next.

A BASIC program for the game of life is given in Figure 7.4, which is a continued figure. The salient points of the program are:

- The array L$ is life's rectangular grid.
- The array N$ is the array for the next generation.
- The rows are numbered from T=1 (top) to B=20 (bottom).
- The columns are numbered from L=1 (left) to R=39 (right).

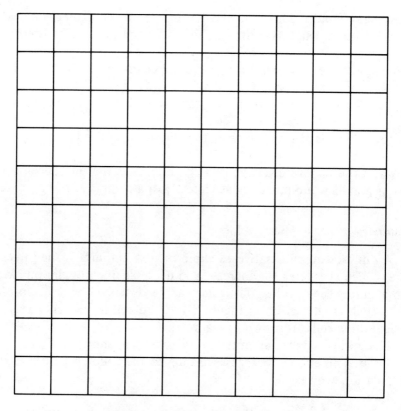

Figure 7.1 Rectangular grid for the game of life.

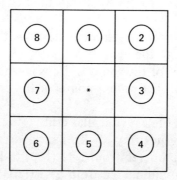

Figure 7.2 Neighboring cells.

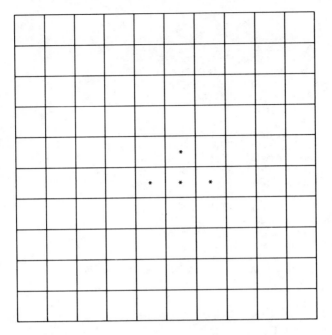

Figure 7.3 An initial configuration for the game of life.

- The x,y points take their normal graphics orientation (see Chapter 1).
- The program counts neighboring cells in the sequence one through eight.
- The program checks for boundaries, that is, top, right side, bottom, and left side.

Figure 7.5 gives a sample run of the program for the game of life.

Many interesting variations to the game of life can be achieved by changing the rules. For example, one frequent variation is to require only two neighbors to generate a birth.

POINT GRAPHICS

Graphic effects can be generated by illuminating appropriate points — usually in color — on the display. Frequently seen examples in posters and publications are busts of Abraham Lincoln and John F. Kennedy. This technique has been used for graphic designs — such as book jackets and a variety of TV commercials.

```
]LIST

5   REM   GAME OF LIFE
10  T = 1:B = 20:L = 1:R = 39
20  T$ = "*": REM   LIFE TOKEN
30  B$ = " ": REM   BACKGROUND
100 DIM L$(B,R),N$(B,R)
199 REM   MAIN LOOP
200 G = 0
210 GOSUB 3000: REM   CLEAR L$
220 GOSUB 4000: REM   ENTER INIT POP
230 GOSUB 5000: REM   DISPLAY L$
240 GOSUB 1000: REM   NEXT GENERATION
250 GOSUB 2000: REM   COPY
260 GOSUB 5000: REM   DISPLAY L$
270 GOSUB 7000: REM   QUERY USER
280 GOTO 240: REM   CONTINUE
999 REM   LOOP THROUGH ARRAY
1000 FOR I = T TO B
1010 FOR J = L TO R
1020 GOSUB 6000: REM   COMPUTE NEIGHBORS
1030 NEXT J
1040 NEXT I
1050 RETURN
1999 REM   COPY N$ -> L$
2000 FOR I = T TO B
2010 FOR J = L TO R
2020 L$(I,J) = N$(I,J)
2030 NEXT J
2040 NEXT I
2050 G = G + 1
2060 RETURN
2999 REM   INIT OLD ARRAY
3000 FOR I = T TO B
3010 FOR J = L TO R
3020 L$(I,J) = B$
3030 NEXT J
3040 NEXT I
3050 RETURN
3999 REM   ENTER INIT POPULATION
4000 HOME
4010 PRINT "ENTER POPULATION AS X,Y PAIR"
4020 PRINT "ENTER 0,0 WHEN FINISHED"
4030 PRINT
4040 PRINT "ENTER NEXT X,Y PAIR"
4050 INPUT X,Y
4060 IF X < > 0 THEN 4090
4070 PRINT "INPUT COMPLETE"
4080 RETURN
4090 IF Y < > 0 THEN 4120
```

Figure 7.4   Program listing for the game of life.

```
4100   PRINT "ERROR"
4110   GOTO 4030
4120 L$(Y,X) = T$
4130   GOTO 4030
5000   HOME
5010   FOR I = T TO B
5020   FOR J = L TO R
5030   PRINT L$(I,J);
5040   NEXT J
5050   PRINT
5060   NEXT I
5070   HTAB 14
5080   PRINT "GENERATION ";G
5090   RETURN
5999   REM  COMPUTE NEIGHBORS
6000 C = 0
6009   REM  POSITION 1
6010   IF I = T THEN 6200
6020   IF L$(I - 1,J) <  > T$ THEN 6100
6030 C = C + 1
6099   REM  POSITION 2
6100   IF J = R THEN 6400
6110   IF L$(I - 1,J + 1) <  > T$ THEN 6200
6120 C = C + 1
6199   REM  POSITION 3
6200   IF J = R THEN 6400
6210   IF L$(I,J + 1) <  > T$ THEN 6300
6220 C = C + 1
6299   REM  POSITION 4
6300   IF I = B THEN 6600
6310   IF L$(I + 1,J + 1) <  > T$ THEN 6400
6320 C = C + 1
6399   REM  POSITION 5
6400   IF I = B THEN 6600
6410   IF L$(I + 1,J) <  > T$ THEN 6500
6420 C = C + 1
6499   REM  POSITION 6
6500   IF J = L THEN 6800
6510   IF L$(I + 1,J - 1) <  > T$ THEN 6600
6520 C = C + 1
6599   REM  POSITION 7
6600   IF J = L THEN 6800
6610   IF L$(I,J - 1) <  > T$ THEN 6700
6620 C = C + 1
6699   REM  POSITION 8
6700   IF I = T THEN 6800
6710   IF L$(I - 1,J - 1) <  > T$ THEN 6800
6720 C = C + 1
6799   REM  SET NEW ARRAY
6800   IF L$(I,J) <  > T$ THEN 6860
```

Figure 7.4   (Continued)

```
6810  IF (C = 2) OR (C = 3) THEN 6840
6820 N$(I,J) = B$
6830  RETURN
6840 N$(I,J) = T$
6850  RETURN
6860  IF C = 3 THEN 6890
6870 N$(I,J) = B$
6880  RETURN
6890 N$(I,J) = T$
6900  RETURN
6999  REM  QUERY USER
7000  GOSUB 8000: REM  CLEAR
7010  VTAB 22
7020  PRINT "CONTINUE?  Y OR N"
7030  INPUT A$
7040  IF A$ = "Y" THEN 7070
7050  PRINT "THATS ALL FOLKS"
7060  GOTO 9999
7070  RETURN
7999  REM  CLEAR LAST 3 LINES
8000  VTAB 22: PRINT
8010  VTAB 23: PRINT
8020  VTAB 24: PRINT
8040  RETURN
9999  END
```

Figure 7.4 (Continued)

Basic Technique

The process of doing point graphics involves the straightforward use of the following low-resolution graphics command:

$$\text{PLOT } x, y$$

However, this command is usually embedded in an easy-to-use user system that requires no programming skill to generate an impressive design.

One approach to point graphics is to visualize the screen as a rectangular array of rectangles, each with a coordinate position. The user is given several functions such as:

PLOT – light up a specified rectangle
ERASE – "unlight" a specified rectangle
RESET – clear the screen for another image

Thus, through a series of interactions with the graphics computer, a collage of colored rectangles is effectively assembled on the screen.

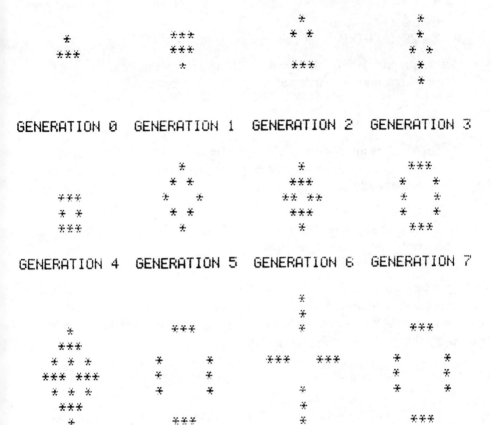

Figure 7.5 Sample run of the game of life.

A second approach is to illuminate rectangles by allowing the user to specify a color, and then enter commands such as:

UP — move up one position and plot in specified color
DOWN — move down one position and plot in specified color
LEFT — move left one position and plot in specified color
RIGHT — move right one position and plot in specified color
ERASE — erase last point
X — set x coordinate
Y — set y coordinate

COLOR – set color
BACKGROUND – set background color

With this approach, the user effectively moves the "cursor" on the screen, creating a visual image.

Illustrative Example – DRAW/1

DRAW/1 is an example of a user-oriented program that generates low-resolution graphics rectangles by requesting that the user specify the following information:

Function
Color – if appropriate
X coordinate – if appropriate
Y coordinate – if appropriate

Upon receiving a line of input, the program executes the specified function immediately, so the user has visual feedback.

The DRAW/1 program is listed as Figure 7.6. The input to the program can take the following forms:

Function	Input
PLOT	$1,c,x,y$
ERASE	$2,0,x,y$
RESET	$3,0,0,0$
QUIT	$4,0,0,0$

where c is a color number, and x and y are screen positions. As an example, the user is asked to enter four numbers, representing one of the above commands, such as:

$$?1,2,20,15$$

The input line represents the plot function (1), the color blue (2), the x coordinate (20), and the y coordinate (15). The program lights up point x,y in the given color. The process continues until the user enters RESET or QUIT. The reset function clears the screen for another image, and the quit function terminates program execution. Figure 7.7 gives a sample input script to DRAW/1. Unfortunately, low-resolution graphics displays cannot be printed.

```
]LIST

5  REM  DRAW/1
10  REM  START
20  GOSUB 5000: REM  DISPLAY MENU
30  REM  DRAW BORDER
40  GOSUB 6000
50  REM  BODY OF DRAW/1
100  GOSUB 7000
110  PRINT "ENTER FCN,COLOR,X,Y"
120  INPUT F,C,X,Y
130  IF F = 1 THEN 190
140  IF F = 2 THEN 220
150  IF F = 3 THEN 20
155  IF F = 4 THEN 250
160  PRINT "ERROR"
170  FOR I = 1 TO 1000: NEXT I
180  GOTO 100
189  REM  PLOT
190  COLOR= C
200  PLOT X - 1,Y - 1
210  GOTO 100
219  REM  ERASE
220  COLOR= 0
230  PLOT X - 1,Y - 1
240  GOTO 100
249  REM  QUIT
250  TEXT
260  HOME
270  PRINT "THATS ALL FOLKS"
280  GOTO 9999
4999  REM  START DRAW/1
5000  TEXT : HOME
5010  VTAB 10
5020  HTAB 15
5030  PRINT "DRAW/1"
5040  PRINT
5050  HTAB 10
5060  PRINT "FUNCTIONS:"
5070  PRINT
5080  HTAB 15
5090  PRINT "PLOT    1,C,X,Y"
5100  HTAB 15
5110  PRINT "ERASE   2,0,X,Y"
5120  HTAB 15
5130  PRINT "RESET   3,0,0,0"
```

Figure 7.6 Program listing of DRAW/1.

```
5140   HTAB 15
5150   PRINT "QUIT    4,0,0,0"
5160   PRINT
5170   HTAB 10
5180   PRINT "PRESS RETURN KEY TO START"
5190   INPUT A$
5200   RETURN
5999   REM  DRAW BORDER
6000   HOME
6010   GR
6020   COLOR= 15
6030   FOR I = 0 TO 39 STEP 2
6040   PLOT 0,I
6050   PLOT I,39
6060   NEXT I
6070   RETURN
6999   REM  CLEAR TEXT AREA
7000   VTAB 21
7010   FOR I = 1 TO 6
7020   PRINT
7030   NEXT I
7040   VTAB 21
7050   RETURN
9999   END
```

Figure 7.6   (Continued)

```
]RUN
               DRAW/1

        FUNCTIONS:

            PLOT    1,C,X,Y
            ERASE   2,0,X,Y
            RESET   3,0,0,0
            QUIT    4,0,0,0

        PRESS RETURN KEY TO START
?



ENTER FCN,COLOR,X,Y
?1,2,20,15
```

Figure 7.7   Sample input script to DRAW/1.

```
ENTER FCN,COLOR,X,Y
?1,11,21,14
```

```
ENTER FCN,COLOR,X,Y
?4,0,0,0
THATS ALL FOLKS
```

Figure 7.7 (Continued)

Illustrative Example — DRAW/2

DRAW/2 is an example of a user-oriented program that generates low-resolution graphics rectangles by utilizing the up-down-left-right approach. The user is permitted to specify the following graphics operations by entering a single keystroke:

Graphics Operation	Keystroke
Move up	U
Move down	D
Move left	L
Move right	R
Set color	C
Erase last point	E
Set background	B
Start over	S
Set x coordinate	X
Set y coordinate	Y
Quit	Q

Four operations request additional information:

Operation	Information Requested
C	Color number
B	Color number
X	X coordinate — a number
Y	Y coordinate — a number

A program listing of DRAW/2 is given in Figure 7.8. The salient points of the program are:

- The "main loop" of the program requests a line of input, which should be a single character. If the letter is one of those mentioned previously, a branch is made to a place in the program to do the specified operation. If an illegal character is entered, it is simply ignored.
- The program checks the boundaries of the screen so the user does not inadvertently cause a program execution-time error.

A sample input script is given as Figure 7.9. As was the case with DRAW/1, low-resolution graphics cannot be displayed.

DRAW/2 is a lot easier to use than DRAW/1. However, the most important aspect of the two programs is that they represent different methods of doing the same thing.

LINE GRAPHICS

The basic idea of line graphics was given in the first chapter, wherein the HLIN and VLIN commands were covered. This chapter gives a technique for drawing lines that are not necessarily horizontal or vertical. Line graphics is important because most geometric shapes are built up from simple lines.

The Problem of Low-Resolution Lines

The basic problem with low-resolution graphics is that when lines are drawn on a rectangular grid, two points on different diagonals do not make a neat line. In Figure 7.10, for example, item (a) forms a neat line while item (b) does not. The approach that is normally taken is to construct a line with both X and Y orientations.

Basic Technique

A straightforward line-drawing algorithm uses the slope formulas given as follows:

$$m = \frac{y_2 - y_1}{x_2 - x_1} \qquad n = \frac{x_2 - x_1}{y_2 - y_1}$$

```
JLIST

5   REM  DRAW/2
10  TEXT : HOME
20  VTAB 10: HTAB 15
30  PRINT "DRAW/2"
40  PRINT
50  PRINT "PRESS RETURN KEY TO START"
60  INPUT A$
70  GOSUB 4000: REM  SET PARAMETERS
80  GOSUB 5000: REM  INITIALIZE
99  REM  START MAIN LOOP
100 GOSUB 6500
110 PRINT "ENTER NEXT COMMAND"
120 INPUT A$
130 IF A$ = "U" THEN 1000
140 IF A$ = "D" THEN 1100
150 IF A$ = "L" THEN 1200
160 IF A$ = "R" THEN 1300
170 IF A$ = "C" THEN 1400
180 IF A$ = "E" THEN 1500
190 IF A$ = "B" THEN 1600
200 IF A$ = "S" THEN 1700
210 IF A$ = "Q" THEN 1800
220 IF A$ = "X" THEN 1900
230 IF A$ = "Y" THEN 2000
240 GOTO 100
999 REM  UP
1000 Y = Y - 1
1010 IF Y > = 0 THEN 3000
1020 Y = 0
1030 GOTO 100
1099 REM  DOWN
1100 Y = Y + 1
1110 IF Y < = 39 THEN 3000
1120 Y = 39
1130 GOTO 100
1199 REM  LEFT
1200 X = X - 1
1210 IF X > = 0 THEN 3000
1220 X = 0
1230 GOTO 100
1299 REM  RIGHT
1300 X = X + 1
1310 IF X < = 39 THEN 3000
1320 X = 39
```

Figure 7.8 Program listing of DRAW/2.

```
1330   GOTO 100
1399   REM   COLOR
1400   PRINT "ENTER NUMBER OF COLOR"
1410   INPUT A
1420   IF (A > = 0) AND (A < = 15) THEN 1440
1430   GOTO 1400
1440   COLOR= A:C = A
1450   GOTO 100
1499   REM   ERASE LAST POINT
1500   COLOR= B
1510   PLOT X,Y
1520   COLOR= C
1530   GOTO 100
1599   REM   BACKGROUND
1600   PRINT "ENTER NUMBER OF COLOR"
1610   INPUT A
1620   IF (A > = 0) AND (A < = 15) THEN 1640
1630   GOTO 1600
1640   B = A
1650   GOTO 100
1699   REM   START OVER
1700   PRINT "START OVER: VERIFY? Y OR N"
1710   INPUT A$
1720   IF A$ = "Y" THEN 80
1730   GOTO 100
1799   REM   QUIT
1800   PRINT "QUIT: VERIFY? Y OR N"
1810   INPUT A$
1820   IF A$ < > "Y" THEN 100
1830   TEXT : HOME
1840   PRINT "SO LONG FOLKS"
1850   GOTO 9999
1899   REM   X COORDINATE
1900   PRINT "ENTER X COORDINATE"
1910   INPUT X
1920   IF (X > = 0) AND (X < = 39) THEN 100
1930   GOTO 1900
1999   REM   Y COORDINATE
2000   PRINT "ENTER Y COORDINATE"
2010   INPUT Y
2020   IF (Y > = 0) AND (Y < = 39) THEN 100
2030   GOTO 2000
2399   REM   PLOT AND CONTINUE
3000   PLOT X,Y
3010   GOTO 100
```

Figure 7.8   (Continued)

```
3999  REM   SET PARAMETERS
4000  C = 15:B = 0
4010  X = 20:Y = 20
4020  RETURN
4999  REM   INITIALIZE
5000  GR
5010  GOSUB 6000: REM   BACKGROUND
5020  COLOR= C
5030  RETURN
5999  REM   BACKGROUND
6000  COLOR= B
6010  FOR I = 0 TO 39
6020  FOR J = 0 TO 39
6030  PLOT I,J
6040  NEXT J
6050  NEXT I
6060  RETURN
6499  REM   CLEAR TEXT AREA
6500  VTAB 21
6510  FOR I = 1 TO 6
6520  PRINT
6530  NEXT I
6540  VTAB 21
6550  RETURN
9999  END
```

Figure 7.8 (Continued)

Then, given a point x with endpoints (x_1, y_1) and (x_2, y_2), a corresponding point y is computed as follows:

$$y = \text{int } (m*(x - x_1) + 0.5) + y_1$$

Similarly, given a point y with the same end points, a corresponding point x is computed as:

$$x = \text{int } (n* (y - y) + 0.5) + x_1$$

In order to obtain a true line in rectangular graphics, it must then be drawn by varying x from x_1 to x_2 and plotting the corresponding y. Then, it must be redrawn by varying y from y_1 to y_2 and plotting the corresponding x.

Figure 7.11 gives a line drawing program that encompasses the concepts given above.

```
]RUN
                    DRAW/2

PRESS RETURN KEY TO START
?
ENTER NEXT COMMAND
?C
ENTER NUMBER OF COLOR
?2
ENTER NEXT COMMAND
?U
ENTER NEXT COMMAND
?U
ENTER NEXT COMMAND
?R
ENTER NEXT COMMAND
?X
ENTER X COORDINATE
?10
ENTER NEXT COMMAND
?Y
ENTER Y COORDINATE
?15
ENTER NEXT COMMAND
?D
ENTER NEXT COMMAND
?L
ENTER NEXT COMMAND
?D
ENTER NEXT COMMAND
?Q
QUIT: VERIFY? Y OR N
?Y
SO LONG FOLKS
```

Figure 7.9   Sample input to DRAW/2.

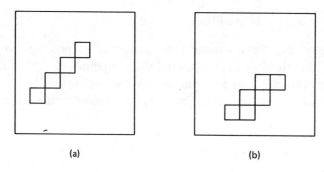

(a)   (b)

Figure 7.10 Diagonal lines on a rectangular grid.

```
]LIST

10   REM   DRAW LINE
20   PRINT "ENTER X1,Y1,X2,Y2"
30   PRINT "ENTER 99,0,0,0 IF DONE"
40   INPUT X1,Y1,X2,Y2
50   IF X1 = 99 THEN 9999
60   HOME : GR : COLOR= 15
70   GOSUB 9000: GOTO 20
8998   REM   DRAW LINE FROM X1,Y1 TO X2,Y2
9000   IF X2 > X1 THEN DX = 1
9010   IF X2 < X1 THEN DX =  - 1
9020   IF X2 = X1 THEN  GOTO 9070
9025 M = (Y2 - Y1) / (X2 - X1)
9030   FOR X = X1 TO X2 STEP DX
9040 Y =  INT ((M * (X - X1)) + .5) + Y1
9050   PLOT X,Y
9060   NEXT X
9070   IF Y2 > Y1 THEN DY = 1
9080   IF Y2 < Y1 THEN DY =  - 1
9090   IF Y2 = Y1 THEN  GOTO 9140
9095 N = (X2 - X1) / (Y2 - Y1)
9100   FOR Y = Y1 TO Y2 STEP DY
9110 X =  INT ((Y - Y1) * N + .5) + X1
9120   PLOT X,Y
9130   NEXT Y
9140   RETURN
9999   END
```

Figure 7.11 Line drawing program.

Illustrative Example — Stereo Effect

An interesting "experiment" in computer graphics is to try to duplicate the stereo effect caused by the manner in which red and green images are processed by the human eye and the brain. This effect can be created on the screen by varying the following parameters:

- Size of cubes
- Separation
- Background color

A schematic of the stereo effect is given in Figure 7.12, and a program listing for a program that does 3-D stereo in red and green is given in Figure 7.13. The idea was brought to the author's attention by an article entitled, "Three-Dimensional Graphics for the Apple II," by Dan Sokol and John Shepard in the November, 1980 issue of *Byte* magazine.

GEOMETRIC SHAPES

In low-resolution computer graphics, useful designs can be constructed with lines, squares, and triangles. Lines were covered previously; squares and triangles are covered here.

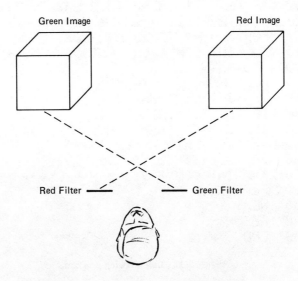

Figure 7.12 Schematic of the stereo effect.

```
]LIST

5   REM   LRES STEREO
10   INPUT "ENTER BACKGROUND COLOR";C
20   INPUT "ENTER SIZE OF CUBE";L
30   INPUT "ENTER SEPARATION";XS
35   REM   COMPUTE CENTERS
40   XL = 20 -   INT ((XS + L +   INT (L / 2)) / 2) - 1
50   XR = XL + XS
60   YL = 20 +   INT ((L +   INT (L / 2)) / 2) - L:YR = YL - 2
65   GR : REM   COLOR BACKGROUND
70   GOSUB 9200
75   REM   DRAW BORDER
80   COLOR= 15: REM   WHITE
90   HLIN 0,39 AT 0
100   VLIN 0,39 AT 39
110   HLIN 39,0 AT 39
120   VLIN 39,0 AT 0
125   REM   SET LEFT COLOR AND DRAW CUBE
130   COLOR= 1: REM   MAGENTA
140   XC = XL:YC = YL: GOSUB 7000
145   REM   SET RIGHT COLOR AND DRAW CUBE
150   COLOR= 12: REM   GREEN
160   XC = XR:YC = YR: GOSUB 7000
170   VTAB 24
180   INPUT "0-STOP, 1-REPEAT ?";A
190   TEXT : HOME
200   IF A = 0 THEN 9998
210   GOTO 10
6998   REM   DRAW CUBE
6999   REM   XC,YC - UPPER LEFT CORNER
7000   ZX = XC:ZY = YC: GOSUB 8000
7010   ZX = XC +   INT (L / 2):ZY = YC -   INT (L / 2)
7020   GOSUB 8000
7030   X1 = XC:Y1 = YC
7040   X2 = X1 +   INT (L / 2):Y2 = Y1 -   INT (L / 2)
7050   GOSUB 9000
7060   X1 = XC + L:Y1 = YC
7070   X2 = X1 +   INT (L / 2):Y2 = Y1 -   INT (L / 2)
7080   GOSUB 9000
7090   X1 = XC:Y1 = YC + L
7100   X2 = X1 +   INT (L / 2):Y2 = Y1 -   INT (L / 2)
7110   GOSUB 9000
7120   X1 = XC + L:Y1 = YC + L
```

Figure 7.13   Low-resolution stereo program.

```
7130 X2 = X1 +  INT (L / 2):Y2 = Y1 -  INT (L / 2)
7140  GOSUB 9000
7150  RETURN
7998  REM  DRAW SQUARE
7999  REM  ZX,ZY - UPPER LEFT CORNER
8000  HLIN ZX,ZX + L AT ZY
8010  VLIN ZY,ZY + L AT ZX + L
8020  HLIN ZX + L,ZX AT ZY + L
8030  VLIN ZY + L,ZY AT ZX
8040  RETURN
8998  REM  ***DRAW LINE***
8999  REM  USES X1,Y1,X2,Y2
9000  IF X2 > X1 THEN DX = 1
9010  IF X2 < X1 THEN DX =  - 1
9020  IF X2 = X1 THEN  GOTO 9070
9025 M = (Y2 - Y1) / (X2 - X1)
9030  FOR X = X1 TO X2 STEP DX
9040 Y =  INT ((M * (X - X1)) + .5) + Y1
9050  PLOT X,Y
9060  NEXT X
9070  IF Y2 > Y1 THEN DY = 1
9080  IF Y2 < Y1 THEN DY =  - 1
9090  IF Y2 = Y1 THEN  GOTO 9140
9095 N = (X2 - X1) / (Y2 - Y1)
9100  FOR Y = Y1 TO Y2 STEP DY
9110 X =  INT (N * (Y - Y1) + .5) + X1
9120  PLOT X,Y
9130  NEXT Y
9140  RETURN
9198  REM  ***BACKGROUND***
9199  REM  USES C
9200  COLOR= C
9210  FOR ROW = 0 TO 39
9220  FOR COL = 0 TO 39
9230  PLOT ROW,COL
9240  NEXT COL
9250  NEXT ROW
9260  RETURN
9998  PRINT "FINI"
9999  END
```

Figure 7.13   (Continued)

Basic Technique

Figure 7.14 gives a set of basic shapes that can easily be programmed using the BASIC language. Each of these shapes requires the following input:

- Height
- x, y coordinate of a key point
- Color

For triangles, a key point is obviously the apex of the triangle. For the square, a key point is the upper left corner. A GOSUB subroutine for each geometric shape is given in Figure 7.15.

Illustrative Example — Art Demo

An example of the use of the low-resolution geometric shapes is given as a "low-resolution art demo" in Figure 7.16. Combined with the program are subroutines to draw lines and set the background

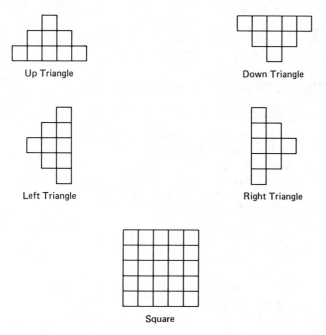

Up Triangle

Down Triangle

Left Triangle

Right Triangle

Square

Figure 7.14   Geometric shapes.

```
]LIST

5   REM   LRES GEOMETRIC SHAPES
10  REM   SUBROUTINE DIRECTORY
12  REM      DNTRIANGLE - 8000
14  REM      UPTRIANGLE - 8200
16  REM      LTRIANGLE  - 8400
18  REM      RTRIANGLE  - 8600
20  REM      SQUARE     - 8800
7998  REM  ***DNTRIANGLE***
7999  REM  USES H,X,Y,C
8000  COLOR= C
8010  PLOT X,Y
8020  IF H < = 1 THEN  RETURN
8030  FOR ROW = 2 TO H
8040  T = ROW - 1
8050  HLIN X - T,X + T AT Y - T
8060  NEXT ROW
8070  RETURN
8198  REM  ***UPTRIANGLE***
8199  REM  USES H,X,Y,C
8200  COLOR= C
8210  PLOT X,Y
8220  IF H < = 1 THEN  RETURN
8230  FOR ROW = 2 TO H
8240  T = ROW - 1
8250  HLIN X - T,X + T AT Y + T
8260  NEXT ROW
8270  RETURN
8398  REM  ***LTRIANGLE***
8399  REM  USES H,X,Y,C
8400  COLOR= C
8410  PLOT X,Y
8420  IF H < = 1 THEN  RETURN
8430  FOR COL = 2 TO H
8440  T = COL - 1
8450  VLIN Y - T,Y + T AT X + T
8460  NEXT COL
8470  RETURN
8598  REM  ***RTRIANGLE***
8599  REM  USES H,X,Y,C
8600  COLOR= C
```

Figure 7.15   A set of GOSUB subroutines for the basic geometric shapes.

```
8610  PLOT X,Y
8620  IF H < = 1 THEN  RETURN
8630  FOR COL = 2 TO H
8640  T = COL - 1
8650  VLIN Y - T,Y + T AT X - T
8660  NEXT COL
8670  RETURN
8798  REM  ***SQUARE***
8799  REM  USES H,X,Y,C
8800  COLOR= C
8810  IF H < = 0 THEN  RETURN
8820  FOR ROW = 1 TO H
8830  T = ROW - 1
8840  HLIN X,X + H - 1 AT Y + T
8850  NEXT ROW
8860  RETURN
```

Figure 7.15 (Continued)

```
]LIST

5  REM  LRES ART DEMO
10  REM  SUBROUTINE DIRECTORY
12  REM    DNTRIANGLE - 8000
14  REM    UPTRIANGLE - 8200
16  REM    LTRIANGLE  - 8400
18  REM    RTRIANGLE  - 8600
20  REM    SQUARE     - 8800
22  REM    LINE       - 9000
24  REM    BACKGROUND - 9200
30  GR
38  REM  DO BACKGROUND
40  C = 8: GOSUB 9200
50  REM  DO BORDER
60  C = 12
70  X1 = 1:Y1 = 1:X2 = 38:Y2 = 1
80  GOSUB 9000
90  X2 = 1:Y2 = 38: GOSUB 9000
100 X1 = 38:Y1 = 38: GOSUB 9000
110 X2 = 38:Y2 = 1: GOSUB 9000
120  REM  DO RTRIANGLE
130 C = 6
140 H = 4:X = 8:Y = 10
150  GOSUB 8600
160  REM  DO LARGE TR
```

Figure 7.16 Low-resolution art demo.

```
170 C = 0
180 X1 = 15:Y1 = 6:X2 = 15:Y2 = 25
190  GOSUB 9000
200 X1 = 15:Y1 = 25:X2 = 25:Y2 = 6
210  GOSUB 9000
220 X1 = 25:Y1 = 6:X2 = 15:Y2 = 6
230  GOSUB 9000
240  REM   DO SQUARE
250 C = 14
260 H = 12:X = 8:Y = 20
270  GOSUB 8800
280  REM   DO UP TRIANGLE
290 C = 0
300 H = 6:X = 30:Y = 20
310  GOSUB 8200
320  REM   DO DOWN TRIANGLE
330 C = 14
340 H = 6:X = 30:Y = 19
350  GOSUB 8000
360  REM   ADD PTS
370  COLOR= 0: PLOT 30,9
380  COLOR= 14: PLOT 30,30
390  GOTO 9999
7998  REM   ***DNTRIANGLE***
7999  REM   USES H,X,Y,C
8000  COLOR= C
8010  PLOT X,Y
8020  IF H <  = 1 THEN  RETURN
8030  FOR ROW = 2 TO H
8040 T = ROW - 1
8050  HLIN X - T,X + T AT Y - T
8060  NEXT ROW
8070  RETURN
8198  REM   ***UPTRIANGLE***
8199  REM   USES H,X,Y,C
8200  COLOR= C
8210  PLOT X,Y
8220  IF H <  = 1 THEN  RETURN
8230  FOR ROW = 2 TO H
8240 T = ROW - 1
8250  HLIN X - T,X + T AT Y + T
8260  NEXT ROW
8270  RETURN
8398  REM   ***LTRIANGLE***
8399  REM   USES H,X,Y,C
8400  COLOR= C
```

Figure 7.16   (Continued)

```
8410  PLOT X,Y
8420  IF H <  = 1 THEN  RETURN
8430  FOR COL = 2 TO H
8440 T = COL - 1
8450  VLIN Y - T,Y + T AT X + T
8460  NEXT COL
8470  RETURN
8598  REM  ***RTRIANGLE***
8599  REM  USES H,X,Y,C
8600  COLOR= C
8610  PLOT X,Y
8620  IF H <  = 1 THEN  RETURN
8630  FOR COL = 2 TO H
8640 T = COL - 1
8650  VLIN Y - T,Y + T AT X - T
8660  NEXT COL
8670  RETURN
8798  REM  ***SQUARE***
8799  REM  USES H,X,Y,C
8800  COLOR= C
8810  IF H <  = 0 THEN  RETURN
8820  FOR ROW = 1 TO H
8830 T = ROW - 1
8840  HLIN X,X + H - 1 AT Y + T
8850  NEXT ROW
8860  RETURN
8998  REM  ***DRAW LINE***
8999  REM  USES X1,Y1,X,Y2,C
9000  COLOR= C
9005  IF X2 > X1 THEN DX = 1
9010  IF X2 < X1 THEN DX =  - 1
9020  IF X2 = X1 THEN  GOTO 9070
9025 M = (Y2 - Y1) / (X2 - X1)
9030  FOR X = X1 TO X2 STEP DX
9040 Y =  INT ((M * (X - X1)) + .5) + Y1
9050  PLOT X,Y
9060  NEXT X
9070  IF Y2 > Y1 THEN DY = 1
9080  IF Y2 < Y1 THEN DY =  - 1
9090  IF Y2 = Y1 THEN  GOTO 9140
9095 N = (X2 - X1) / (Y2 - Y1)
9100  FOR Y = Y1 TO Y2 STEP DY
9110 X =  INT (N * (Y - Y1) + .5) + X1
9120  PLOT X,Y
9130  NEXT Y
9140  RETURN
```

Figure 7.16   (Continued)

```
9198  REM   ***BACKGROUND***
9199  REM   USES C
9200  COLOR= C
9210  FOR ROW = 0 TO 39
9220  FOR COL = 0 TO 39
9230  PLOT ROW,COL
9240  NEXT COL
9250  NEXT ROW
9260  RETURN
9999  END
```

Figure 7.16 (Continued)

color. The program creates a so-called art demonstration by making successive calls to the various GOSUB subroutines, explained above. The program demonstrates a useful technique, wherein subroutines are developed for use by relatively inexperienced persons who may be at the initial learning stage of the BASIC language.

CURVES

Low-resolution graphics does not lend itself to the display of plane curves. While conventional mathematical techniques certainly apply, the visual fidelity of low-resolution graphics is not in general sufficient to generate a neat image.

Basic Technique

With low-resolution graphics, geometric distances must fall within screen boundaries. As a result, amplitudes, radii and other displacements are in the range of 0 to 39. Angular measurements are independent of resolution, so the mathematics that customarily apply to high-resolution graphics also apply here.

Illustrative Example – Circle Program

A graphics program that draws circles uses the trigonometry given in Figure 7.17. The algorithm steps through the circle in specified increments, given in degrees. Given a value in degrees, it is converted to radians needed for the computer with a statement of the form:

$$T = A/57.3$$

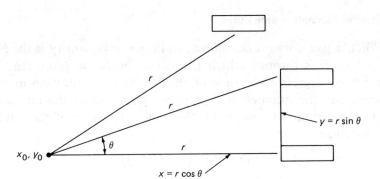

Figure 7.17 Construction of the circle.

The Δx and Δy are then computed as:

$$X=R*COS(T)+.5$$
$$Y=R*SIN(T)+.5$$

where R is the radius and the .5 is added to compensate for rounding. Figure 7.18 gives the low-resolution circle program.

```
]LIST

5   REM  LRES CIRCLE
10  GR
20  COLOR= 2
30  PRINT "ENTER CENTER AS X,Y"
40  INPUT X0,Y0
50  PRINT "ENTER RADIUS AND ANGLE"
60  INPUT R,D
70  FOR A = 0 TO 360 STEP D
80 T = A / 57.3
90 X = R *  COS (T) + .5
100 Y = R *  SIN (T) + .5
110  PLOT X0 + X,Y0 + Y
120  NEXT A
130  END
```

Figure 7.18 Circle program.

Illustrative Example — Sine Curve

When a sine curve is computed, an important quantity is the number of degrees through which the curve should be projected. The number of degrees must then be divided by the resolution in order to compute the number of degrees per point. Once the number of degrees per point is computed, then the amplitude of the curve is computed as:

$$Y=R*SIN(A*X/57.3)$$

where:

X is the point on the x axis
A is the number of degrees per point
57.3 is the conversion factor of degrees to radians

A schematic of the construction of a sine curve is given as Figure 7.19, and the sine curve program is given as Figure 7.20.

One characteristic of low-resolution curves is that they are distorted in the ratio of approximately $\frac{x}{y} :: \frac{5}{7}$. Thus, the circle and sine curves appear slightly flat. Compensation can be achieved by multiplying x displacements by the ratio 7/5.

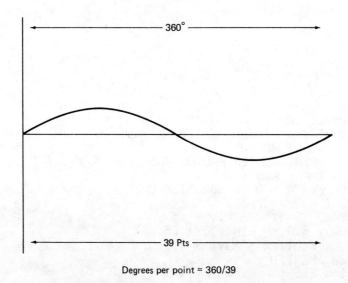

Degrees per point = 360/39

Figure 7.19 Construction of a sine curve.

```
]LIST

5   REM  LRES SINE CURVE
10  GR
20  COLOR= 15
30  VLIN 0,39 AT 0
40  HLIN 0,39 AT 20
50  PRINT "ENTER AMPLITUDE AND PHASE"
60  INPUT R,D
70  A = D / 39
80  FOR X = 0 TO 39
90  Y = R *  SIN (A * X / 57.3)
100  PLOT X,20 - Y
110  NEXT X
```

Figure 7.20 Sine curve program.

TECHNICAL NOTE

A comment is in order on the version of the BASIC language used in the programs of this and succeeding chapters. First, to reduce the length of some programs, statements are combined on the same line and separated by the colon (:) character. Secondly, the IF statement in some programs contains another executable statement in its body as follows:

IF condition THEN statement

Thus, the statement

IF A>B THEN GOTO 1234

for example, is equivalent to

IF A>B THEN 1234

The additional statement is not restricted to the GOTO statement. As examples, the following statements would be valid:

IF A>B THEN RETURN
IF X>39 THEN X=39

In most versions of BASIC, the word GOTO is interchangeable with THEN in the following context:

IF condition GOTO statement-number

as in

$$\text{IF A>B GOTO 1234}$$

The best source of specific operational information on the BASIC language is available from the reference manual for a particular computer.

VOCABULARY LIST

Knowledge of the following terms will assist the reader in becoming familiar with low-resolution graphics:

Line graphics
Point graphics
Slope graphics
Text graphics

EXERCISES

1. In text graphics, what device serves as the graphic output device?
2. In text graphics, an image is stored as an array of _____ .
3. In point graphics, the two approaches to image construction are _____ _____ and _____ .
4. In line graphics, minimal distortion is achieved by _____ .
5. Routines for generating geometric shapes are implemented with _____ _____ .
6. In drawing curves in low-resolution graphics, distances are determined by _____ .

ANSWERS

1. The printer.
2. Characters.
3. x,y coordinate specification and directional movement.
4. Varying both x and y during image generation.
5. GOSUB subroutines.
6. The size of the screen in number of points.

High-Resolution Graphics

High-resolution graphics combines the simplicity of vector-stroke graphics with the convenience and low cost of raster graphics. High-resolution graphics is considerably more powerful than low-resolution graphics. However, high-resolution graphics facilities are extremely easy to use, so our interest here in the subject matter will primarily cover graphics applications.

TECHNICAL CONCEPTS

The technical aspects of high-resolution graphics were introduced in the first chapter. It is particularly important to emphasize, however, that the high-resolution facilities covered here use raster-scan techniques. On the other hand, the computer can be programmed as though vector-stroke techniques were being used.

Resolution

The graphics computer we are using as a reference model in this book has a resolution of 280 X 160 high-resolution points. This means that the high-resolution screen is 280 points wide and 160 points high. Accordingly, the coordinates are numbered 0 through 279 and 0 through 159, respectively.

161

Graphics Programming

As covered in the first chapter, high-resolution graphics programming requires only three commands (or statements, as the case may be):

HGR

HCOLOR

HPLOT

Clearly, HGR puts the system in the high-resolution graphics mode and HCOLOR sets the high-resolution color.

The HPLOT command can take several related forms:

Case 1: HPLOT x, y
Explanation: This form plots the point x, y.

Case 2: HPLOT x_1, y_1 TO x_2, y_2
Explanation: This form plots a line from (x_1, y_1) to (x_2, y_2).

Case 3: HPLOT TO x_2, y_2
Explanation: This form plots a line from the previous point to (x_2, y_2).

Case 4: HPLOT x_1, y_1 TO x_2, y_2 TO x_3, y_3
Explanation: This form plots lines from (x_1, y_1) to (x_2, y_2) and from (x_2, y_2) to (x_3, y_3).

Case 5: HPLOT TO x_2, y_2 TO x_3, y_3
Explanation: This form plots the lines from the previous point to (x_2, y_2) and from (x_2, y_2) to (x_3, y_3).

Case 6: HPLOT x_i, y_i TO x_j, y_j . . .
Explanation: As covered above, (x_i, y_i) can be omitted. In general, as many instances of TO x_j, y_j can be added to a line as necessary.

where all x_n, y_n can be expressions.

Thus,

HPLOT A,B

HPLOT TO C,D

is equivalent to

HPLOT A, B TO C, D

Similarly,

HPLOT A, B TO C, D TO E, F

is equivalent to

HPLOT A, B TO C, D
HPLOT C, D TO E, F

Refresh Memory

When an HPLOT command is executed, it causes points to be set in the high-resolution page of the refresh memory. If a line has been specified, then a "line of points" is established. Once the points have been set, the video circuitry takes over and an image is generated on the display screen.

Some computers incorporate more than one page of high-resolution refresh memory. However, in this book only one page is considered.

Combined High-Resolution and Low-Resolution Programming

It is possible for a graphics program to alternate between the high-resolution and low-resolution graphics modes without user intervention. In fact, Figure 8.1 gives an example of a case where it is done.

For programs written in the BASIC language without machine-dependent facilities, the image must be redrawn for each frame be-

```
]LIST

5   INPUT N
10  GR
20  COLOR= 15
30  VLIN 0,39 AT 20
40  HLIN 0,39 AT 20
50  FOR I = 1 TO N: NEXT I
60  HGR
70  HCOLOR= 3
80  HPLOT 5,5 TO 250,150
90  HPLOT 5,150 TO 250,5
100 FOR I = 1 TO N: NEXT I
110 GOTO 10
```

Figure 8.1 An example of alternating between the high- and low-resolution graphics modes.

cause the GR and HGR commands clear their respective pages in refresh memory.

It is possible to alternate between the modes without image redraw, but special features of a particular computer are needed.

LINE DRAWINGS

High-resolution graphics is essentially a matter of drawing points and lines. If the points are close enough, the visual appearance is that of a line. When a line is plotted with the HPLOT command, adjacent points, comprising the line, are drawn so the resolution is as good as it can be.

High-Resolution Stereo

The stereo effect introduced for low-resolution graphics provides an excellent example of line drawings in high-resolution graphics. The program is similar in concept to the low-resolution version, except that high-resolution facilities are used. However, with high-resolution graphics, a hard copy of the screen can be generated. It is shown in Figure 8.2. The program is listed in Figure 8.3.

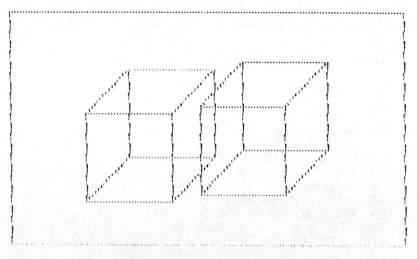

Figure 8.2 High-resolution stereo image.

```
]LIST

5   REM   HRES STEREO
20  INPUT "ENTER SIZE OF CUBE";L
30  INPUT "ENTER SEPARATION";XS
32  INPUT "ENTER Y DISPLACEMENT";DY
35  REM   COMPUTE CENTERS
40 XL = 140 -  INT ((XS + L +  INT (L / 2)) / 2)
50 XR = XL + XS
60 YL = 80 +  INT ((L +  INT (L / 2)) / 2) - L:YR = YL - DY
65  HGR
75  REM   DRAW BORDER
80  COLOR= 3: REM    WHITE
90  HPLOT 1,1 TO 279,1
100  HPLOT  TO 279,159
110  HPLOT  TO 1,159
120  HPLOT  TO 1,1
125  REM   SET LEFT COLOR AND DRAW CUBE
130  HCOLOR= 5: REM    RED
140 XC = XL:YC = YL: GOSUB 7000
145  REM   SET RIGHT COLOR AND DRAW CUBE
150  HCOLOR= 1: REM    GREEN
160 XC = XR:YC = YR: GOSUB 7000
170  VTAB 24
180  INPUT "0-STOP, 1-REPEAT ?";A
190  TEXT : HOME
200  IF A = 0 THEN  PRINT "FINI": END
210  GOTO 20
6998  REM   DRAW CUBE
6999  REM   XC,YC - UPPER LEFT CORNER
7000 ZX = XC:ZY = YC: GOSUB 8000
7010 ZX = XC +  INT (L / 2):ZY = YC -  INT (L / 2)
7020  GOSUB 8000
7030 X1 = XC:Y1 = YC
7040 X2 = X1 +  INT (L / 2):Y2 = Y1 -  INT (L / 2)
7050  HPLOT X1,Y1 TO X2,Y2
7060 X1 = XC + L:Y1 = YC
7070 X2 = X1 +  INT (L / 2):Y2 = Y1 -  INT (L / 2)
7080  HPLOT X1,Y1 TO X2,Y2
7090 X1 = XC:Y1 = YC + L
7100 X2 = X1 +  INT (L / 2):Y2 = Y1 -  INT (L / 2)
7110  HPLOT X1,Y1 TO X2,Y2
7120 X1 = XC + L:Y1 = YC + L
7130 X2 = X1 +  INT (L / 2):Y2 = Y1 -  INT (L / 2)
7140  HPLOT X1,Y1 TO X2,Y2
7150  RETURN
7998  REM   DRAW SQUARE
7999  REM   ZX,ZY - UPPER LEFT CORNER
8000  HPLOT ZX,ZY TO ZX + L,ZY
8010  HPLOT  TO ZX + L,ZY + L
8020  HPLOT  TO ZX,ZY + L
8030  HPLOT  TO ZX,ZY
8040  RETURN
```

Figure 8.3 High-resolution stereo program.

White Noise

One means of illustrating the usefulness of a system that facilitates the plotting of lines is to consider the visual effect of generating an image by choosing the end points of a set of lines along with their color at random. This could be regarded as visualization of "white noise." More specifically, a program to produce visual white noise would include the following steps:

- Select x_1 and x_2 at random in the range of 0 to 279.
- Select y_1 and y_2 at random in the range of 0 to 159.
- Select a color at random in the range of 0 to 7.
- Plot a line from (x_1, y_1) to (x_2, y_2) in the randomly selected color.
- Save the line segment in an array for later erasure when the number of lines on the screen reaches a specified limit.

Randomly selected lines are stored successively until corresponding arrays are filled. Then as new lines are generated, old ones are erased by replotting them in the background color. Figure 8.4 gives an illustrative example of visual white noise, and Figure 8.5 gives the program to generate the visual image.

The *idea* for the visual white noise program was mentioned in a two-page article by Louis Cesa in *Byte* magazine. The reference is given in the next section.

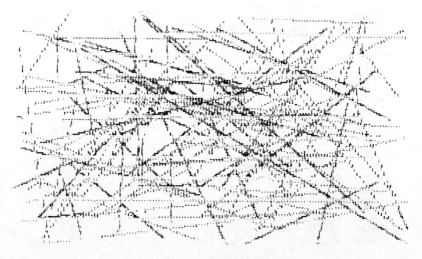

Figure 8.4 Visual white noise.

String Art

An unusual linear effect can be displayed by randomly moving end points across the screen. Color, number of line segments, and length of line segments are chosen at random. As in the preceding example, line segments are stored until a specified limit is reached, and then older segments are erased. The visual result is surprisingly similar to

```
]LIST

10   REM   WHITE NOISE
20   DIM X1(200),X2(200),Y1(200),Y2(200)
30   REM   INITIALIZE VARIABLES
40   X1 = 0:X2 = 0:Y1 = 0:Y2 = 0
50   REM   INPUT PARAMETERS
60   INPUT "NUMBER OF LINES";N
70   INPUT "NUMBER OF REPLICATIONS";L
80   REM   SET HIRES GRAPHICS MODE
90   HGR
100  REM   REPLICATE "L" TIMES
110  FOR Z9 = 1 TO L
120  REM   DRAW "N" LINES
130  FOR I = 1 TO N
140  REM   ERASE OLD LINE
150  HCOLOR= 0
160  HPLOT X1(I),Y1(I) TO X2(I),Y2(I)
170  REM   RANDOM COLOR
190  TC% = 1 + 7 * RND (1)
210  REM   CHOOSE RANDOM END POINTS
220  X1 = RND (1) * 279
230  X2 = RND (1) * 279
240  Y1 = RND (1) * 159
250  Y2 = RND (1) * 159
300  REM   PLOT LINES
310  HCOLOR= TC%
320  HPLOT X1,Y1 TO X2,Y2
330  REM   STORE POINTS
340  X1(I) = X1:X2(I) = X2
350  Y1(I) = Y1:Y2(I) = Y2
360  NEXT I
370  NEXT Z9
375  TEXT : HOME
380  VTAB 24: PRINT "THAT'S ALL FOLKS"
390  END
```

Figure 8.5 Program to generate visual white noise.

kinetic string art, as exemplified in Figure 8.6. The corresponding program is given in Figure 8.7.

The program represents a modified form of an *algorithm* given by Louis Cesa in an article entitled "Kinetic String Art for the Apple," published in *Byte*, November, 1980, pages 62–63.

CURVES

In high-resolution graphics, curves are generated by drawing successive points that have a curvilinear relationship. In most cases, a mathematical formula is used to generate a given curve, even though the points may be connected with line segments to form a geometric figure.

The Circle

A diagram for computing the points of a circle was given in Chapter 7, for low-resolution graphics. The concept is the same even though the results are strikingly dissimilar, as shown in Figure 8.8. The program is listed in Figure 8.9.

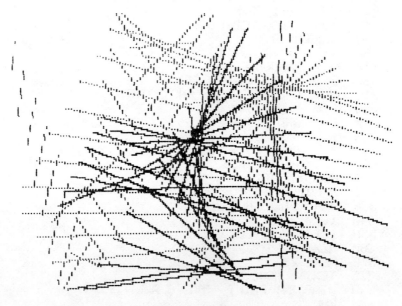

Figure 8.6   String art.

```
]LIST

10   REM   STRING ART PROGRAM
20   DIM X1(200),X2(200),Y1(200),Y2(200),DX(2),DY(2)
30   REM   INITIALIZE VARIABLES
40   X1 = 0:X2 = 0:Y1 = 0:Y2 = 0:NC% = 0:ND% = 0
50   REM   INPUT PARAMETERS
60   INPUT "NUMBER OF LINES";N
70   INPUT "NUMBER OF REPLICATIONS";L
72   INPUT "LENGTH OF LINE SEGMENT";LS
74   INPUT "CHANGE FREQUENCY";CF
80   REM   SET HIRES GRAPHICS MODE
90   HGR
100  REM   REPLICATE "L" TIMES
110  FOR Z9 = 1 TO L
120  REM   DRAW "N" LINES
130  FOR I = 1 TO N
140  REM   ERASE OLD LINE
150  HCOLOR= 0
160  HPLOT X1(I),Y1(I) TO X2(I),Y2(I)
170  REM   RANDOM COLOR
180  IF NC% < > 0 THEN 220
190  TC% = 1 + 7 * RND (1)
200  NC% = CF * (1 + RND (1))
210  REM   RANDOM "DX" AND "DY"
220  IF ND% < > 0 THEN 290
230  DX(1) = LS * RND (1) - .4 * LS
240  DX(2) = LS * RND (1) - .4 * LS
250  DY(1) = LS * RND (1) - .4 * LS
260  DY(2) = LS * RND (1) - .4 * LS
270  ND% = CF * (1 + RND (1))
280  REM   COMPUTE X'S AND Y'S
290  GOSUB 9000
300  REM   PLOT LINES
310  HCOLOR= TC%
320  HPLOT X1,Y1 TO X2,Y2
325  NC% = NC% - 1:ND% = ND% - 1
330  REM   STORE POINTS
340  X1(I) = X1:X2(I) = X2
350  Y1(I) = Y1:Y2(I) = Y2
360  NEXT I
370  NEXT Z9
375  TEXT : HOME
380  VTAB 24: PRINT "THAT'S ALL FOLKS"
390  END
8998 REM   COMPUTE X'S AND Y'S
```

Figure 8.7   Program to generate string art.

```
9000 TX = X1 + DX(1)
9010  IF TX > = 0 AND TX < = 279 THEN 9030
9020 TX = X1:DX(1) = - DX(1)
9030 X1 = TX
9040 TX = X2 + DX(2)
9050  IF TX > = 0 AND TX < = 279 THEN 9070
9060 TX = X2:DX(2) = - DX(2)
9070 X2 = TX
9080 TY = Y1 + DY(1)
9090  IF TY > = 0 AND TY < = 191 THEN 9110
9100 TY = Y1:DY(1) = - DY(1)
9110 Y1 = TY
9120 TY = Y2 + DY(2)
9130  IF TY > = 0 AND TY < = 191 THEN 9150
9140 TY = Y2:DY(2) = - DY(2)
9150 Y2 = TY
9160  RETURN
```

Figure 8.7   (Continued)

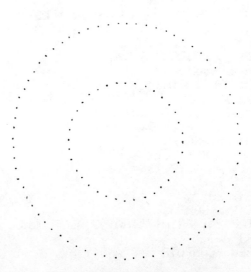

Figure 8.8   High-resolution circles.

```
]LIST
5  REM  HRES CIRCLE
6  K = 180 / 3.14159
10  HGR
20  HCOLOR= 3
30  INPUT "ENTER RADIUS AND ANGLE";R,DA
40  X0 = 140:Y0 = 80
50  FOR A = 0 TO 360 STEP DA
60  TH = A / K
70  X1 = R *  COS (TH)
80  Y1 = R *  SIN (TH)
90  HPLOT X0 + X1,Y0 + Y1
95  NEXT A
99  GOTO 30
```

Figure 8.9 Program to generate high-resolution circles.

If a small angle (such as 10°) is entered, then many points on the circumference of the circle are generated and the resulting figure appears as a true circle, even though the points are not connected. If a larger angle (such as 60°) is entered, then a certain amount of imagination is needed to visualize the curve. As the radius becomes smaller, a larger angle can be entered and still achieve reasonably good visual fidelity.

The Polygon

Conceptually, a polygon is generated if the points are connected in the circle program, presented in the previous section. Given that the number of sides in the polygon is entered as an input parameter, then the angle between points is computed as:

$$d = (a_2 - a_1)/n$$

where a_2 and a_1 are the ending and starting angles, respectively — usually taken as 360° and 0° — and n is the number of sides. The program executes by plotting the initial point as

$$\text{HPLOT } x_0 + r_1 \, y_0$$

where r is the radius, and then draws the sides of the polygon with statements of the form:

$$\text{HPLOT TO } x_0 + r \cos (\theta)_1 \, y_0 + r \sin (\theta)$$

where θ is the angle in radians. A set of inscribed polygons generated graphically is given in Figure 8.10, and the program used to generate them is given in Figure 8.11.

The Sine Curve

The key concept in displaying a sine curve image is determining the number of degrees between points on the x axis. This is achieved

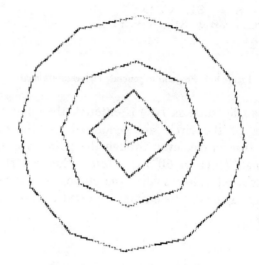

Figure 8.10 High-resolution polygons.

```
]LIST

5   REM   HRES POLYGON
6   HGR : HCOLOR= 3
10  PI = 3.14159
20  A1 = 0:A2 = 2 * PI
25  X0 = 140:Y0 = 80
30   INPUT "NUMBER OF SIDES";N
40   INPUT "RADIUS OF POLYGON";R
60  D = (A2 - A1) / N
70   HPLOT X0 + R,Y0
80   FOR TH = A1 TO A2 + .01 STEP D
90   HPLOT  TO X0 + R *  COS (TH),Y0 + R *  SIN (TH)
95   NEXT TH
99   GOTO 30
```

Figure 8.11 Program to generate high-resolution polygons.

by dividing the phase by the x-axis resolution. This "angle" is computed as:

$$a=d/279$$

For example, if the phase (d) is 360°, then a would be equal to 1.29° for high-resolution graphics for positive x values. Thus, for each point, as x ranges from 0 to 279, an expression for the angle is given and converted to radians as:

$$A*X/57.3$$

and the y coordinate is computed as:

$$Y=R*SIN(A*X/57.3)$$

where R is the amplitude of the sine curve. A sample sine curve is given in Figure 8.12, and the corresponding program is given in Figure 8.13.

It is important to observe in the high-resolution sine curve program that we always plot (x,y) points, and accordingly convert coordinates to angular measure only if it is required by the mathematical formula.

CHARACTER GENERATION

In many small graphics computers, the text and high-resolution graphics modes cannot be used at the same time. This is certainly not a

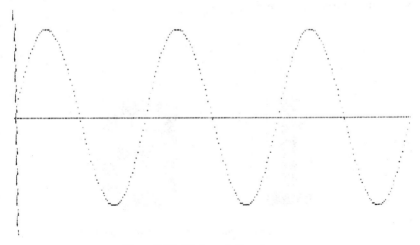

Figure 8.12   High-resolution sine curve.

```
]LIST

5   REM   HRES SINE CUVE
10   HGR
20   HCOLOR= 3
30   HPLOT 1,1 TO 1,159
40   HPLOT 1,80 TO 279,80
45   VTAB 21
50   PRINT "ENTER AMPLITUDE AND PHASE"
60   INPUT R,D
70   A = D / 279
80   FOR X = 0 TO 279
90   Y = R * SIN (A * X / 57.3)
100   HPLOT X,80 - Y
110   NEXT X
```

Figure 8.13   Program to generate a high-resolution sine curve.

universal characteristic of computers with graphics capability, but it is common enough to warrant special attention. If it is desirable to present text characters together with a high-resolution image in a graphics display, then the text mode characters have to be generated by using high-resolution graphics techniques.

Models of two text mode characters are given in Figure 8.14. As such, the models are identical to the 5 X 7-dot matrix positions given for text characters in Chapter 1. All that is needed to generate a character of this type is to specify a consistently placed (x,y) point for character relocation and to write a GOSUB subroutine for each text mode character to be displayed.

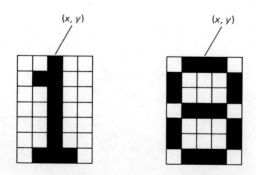

Figure 8.14   Models of characters for character generation.

The program listed in Figure 8.15 contains a GOSUB subroutine for each of the characters displayed in Figure 8.14. Through the use of the (x, y) coordinate point, a text mode character can be located in any position on the display screen. Figure 8.16 gives an example of character generation.

```
]LIST

5   REM   CHARACTER GENERATION EXAMPLE
10    HGR
20    HCOLOR= 3
30    HPLOT 128,70 TO 159,70 TO 159,96 TO 128,96 TO 128,70
40    X = 140:Y = 80
50    GOSUB 1000
60    X = 147:Y = 80
70    GOSUB 8000
80    GOTO 9999
999   REM   GENERATE "1"
1000    HPLOT X,Y TO X,Y + 6
1010    HPLOT X - 1,Y + 1
1020    HPLOT X - 1,Y + 6 TO X + 1,Y + 6
1030    RETURN
7999   REM   GENERATE "8"
8000    HPLOT X - 1,Y TO X + 1,Y
8010    HPLOT X - 2,Y + 1 TO X - 2,Y + 2
8020    HPLOT X + 2,Y + 1 TO X + 2,Y + 2
8030    HPLOT X - 1,Y + 3 TO X + 1,Y + 3
8040    HPLOT X - 2,Y + 4 TO X - 2,Y + 5
8050    HPLOT X + 2,Y + 4 TO X + 2,Y + 5
8060    HPLOT X - 1,Y + 6 TO X + 1,Y + 6
8070    RETURN
9999    END
```

Figure 8.15   A program that generates text mode characters in high-resolution mode.

Figure 8.16   Characters generated with the character generator program.

VOCABULARY LIST

Knowledge of the following terms will help the reader in gaining a good grasp of high-resolution graphics:

Character generation
HCOLOR
HGR
HPLOT

EXERCISES

1. Simplify the following statements:

$$\text{HPLOT A,B TO A+13, B-1}$$
$$\text{HPLOT A+13,B-1 TO C-14, 2*D-1}$$

2. When low-resolution and high-resolution graphics are combined in an alternating manner, why is it necessary to redraw the figures, since the images exist in separate places in refresh memory?

ANSWERS

1. HPLOT A,G TO A+13,B-1 TO C-14, 24D-1.
2. It is necessary because the GR and HGR commands clear their respective areas of refresh memory.

Principles of Animation

Many persons commonly associate animation with computer graphics — probably because of the influence of traditional television programming and more recently, TV games. Most large department stores demonstrate some forms of TV games. Clearly, not all TV games use computers, and many are built into electronic circuitry. Regardless, the result is very dramatic, even though there is more to computer graphics than animation. Thus far, the primary interest of the outside world in computer animation has been in the area of entertainment. The potential of computer animation for business and professional people has yet to be explored.

BASIC TECHNIQUE

The basic technique of computer animation involves the following steps:

- Display a visual image
- Displace one or more of the pixels that comprise the image
- Move the image to a "new" location, replacing the displaced pixels
- Erase the "old" image, if necessary

Certainly, there are other issues in computer animation, but the above list essentially summarizes the basic technique that is involved.

Principal One — Displacement

Figure 9.1 gives a program in low-resolution graphics that moves a bullet across the screen. Two variables,[1] XLEFT and XRIGHT, effectively move across the screen until the right boundary is reached. Then the process repeats starting with the leftmost boundary. At each new position, the bullet is drawn and the previous bullet is erased. The program demonstrates the following principle:

Displacement Principle: When moving an image, draw the "new" image before erasing the "old" image.

In some cases, especially ones in which the images overlap, it is not possible to completely erase the old image because some of the new image would be erased as well. When this occurs, pixels have to be selectively erased.

```
]LIST

5   REM  BULLET PROGRAM - CONSTANT SPEED
10  HOME
20  PRINT "ENTER COLOR AND REPETITIONS"
30  INPUT C,L
40 DX = 1: REM  DELTA X
50  FOR I = 1 TO L
60  HOME : GR
70 XLEFT = 0: PLOT XLEFT,20
80 XRIGHT = XLEFT + DX
90  IF XRIGHT > 39 THEN 160
100  COLOR= C
110  PLOT XRIGHT,20
120  COLOR= 0
130  PLOT XLEFT,20
140 XLEFT = XRIGHT
150  GOTO 80
160  NEXT I
170  TEXT : HOME
180  PRINT "END OF BULLET PROGRAM"
999  END
```

Figure 9.1 Bullet program demonstrating the displacement principle.

---

[1] In this version of BASIC, only the leftmost two characters of a variable name are significant to the computer.

Principle Two — Speed

In the previous bullet program, the image moves at a constant speed across the screen. In fact, a delta x (i.e., DX in lines 40 and 80) of one is the increment in the x direction for animated movement. In Figure 9.2, which is a modification of the first bullet program, delta x (i.e., DX in lines 40, 55, and 80) increases by one for each pass through the loop. This gives the illusion of an increase in speed and demonstrates the following principle:

Speed Principle: To project the illusion of speed in an animated sequence, increase the distance between successive images as animation time increases.

In some cases, an increased distance between images will result in a lower number of screen images per frame. When this occurs, it is necessary to also move the location of the first image projected on the screen to enhance the illusionary sensation of movement.

```
]LIST

5   REM  BULLET PROGRAM - SPEED INCREASES
10  HOME
20  PRINT "ENTER COLOR AND REPETITIONS"
30  INPUT C,L
40  DX = 0: REM  DELTA X INITIAL VALUE
50  FOR I = 1 TO L
55  DX = DX + 1: REM  INCREASE SPEED
60  HOME : GR
70  XLEFT = 0: PLOT XLEFT,20
80  XRIGHT = XLEFT + DX
90  IF XRIGHT > 39 THEN 160
100  COLOR= C
110  PLOT XRIGHT,20
120  COLOR= 0
130  PLOT XLEFT,20
140 XLEFT = XRIGHT
150  GOTO 80
160  NEXT I
170  TEXT : HOME
180  PRINT "END OF BULLET PROGRAM"
999  END
```

Figure 9.2 Modified bullet program demonstrating the speed principle.

LOW-RESOLUTION ANIMATION

The basic techniques of animated graphics were given in the preceding section. This section gives several examples that provide a variety of programming hints in a context of real-life applications.

Illustrative Example — Moving Bird Program

Figure 9.3 gives a schematic of a bird that "flies off the screen." The action is accomplished in two moves. In move 1, the wings are raised, and in move 2, the body is raised to the level of the wings. Even though this is a very simple example, two key points can be emphasized:

- The image must have an (x,y) position. In Figure 9.3, the (x,y) point is denoted with a dot.
- A delay is needed so the user can visualize the image.

The "moving bird" program is listed in Figure 9.4. Animation is achieved by moving the image in the y direction with a FOR loop. (The reader should note, for example, statements numbered 70 through 100 in the program.)

Illustrative Example — Moving Dog Program

Figure 9.5 gives a schematic of a dog that moves from left to right on the screen. The example is only slightly more complicated than the moving bird program. As before, the animation is achieved by

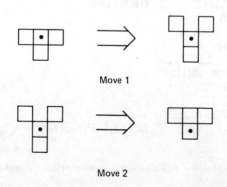

Move 1

Move 2

Figure 9.3   Moves in an elementary animation sequence.

```
JLIST

5   REM   MOVING BIRD PROGRAM
10    PRINT "ENTER COLOR, FREQUENCY, AND DELAY"
20    INPUT C,N,D
30    FOR I = 1 TO N
40    HOME : GR
50    X = 20:Y = 38: GOSUB 3000: REM   SETUP
60    GOSUB 4000: REM   DELAY
70    FOR Y = 38 TO 2 STEP  - 1
80    GOSUB 1000: GOSUB 4000: REM   MOVE 1 AND DELAY
90    GOSUB 2000: GOSUB 4000: REM   MOVE 2 AND DELAY
100   NEXT Y
110   NEXT I
120   TEXT : HOME
130   PRINT "END OF PROGRAM"
140   GOTO 9999
999   REM   MOVE 1
1000    COLOR= C: PLOT X - 1,Y - 1: PLOT X + 1,Y - 1
1010    COLOR= 0: PLOT X - 1,Y: PLOT X + 1,Y
1020    RETURN
1999    REM   MOVE 2
2000    COLOR= C: PLOT X,Y - 1
2010    COLOR= 0: PLOT X,Y + 1
2020    RETURN
2999    REM   SETUP
3000    COLOR= C
3010    HLIN X - 1,X + 1 AT Y
3020    PLOT X,Y + 1
3030    RETURN
3999    REM   DELAY
4000    FOR Z = 1 TO D: NEXT Z
4010    RETURN
9999    END
```

Figure 9.4   Listing of the moving bird program demonstrating low-resolution animation.

two moves: move 1 transforms the appendages and move 2 brings the body along, as demonstrated in Figure 9.6. This program also has an (x, y) orientation, and a limited sensation of speed can be generated by reducing or increasing the delay time. Figure 9.7 gives a program listing of the moving dog program.

Illustrative Example — Jumping Jack Program

A commonly known exercise among athletes is the "jumping jacks," wherein a person's arms and legs move inward and outward in a

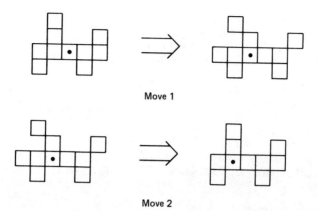

Move 1

Move 2

Figure 9.5 Basic moves in the moving dog program.

rhythmic motion, as shown in Figure 9.8. This is a dramatic example because the number of repetitions and the speed can be entered by the user — just as one would do in real life. This program, listed in Figure 9.9, gives no (x, y) movement, but the arms, legs, and head move. Careful analysis of the program will uncover symmetry in the way the arms and legs are moved in close time proximity to each other in order to add realism to the animation.

HIGH-RESOLUTION ANIMATION

The inherent speed of high-resolution graphics permits more freedom in choosing how an image is drawn. For example, an image can be completely erased before it is redrawn, with good results.

Basic Technique

Since a high-resolution image is usually constructed as a set of points that are connected in a meaningful manner, it is useful to store the points arrays X and Y, for example, and loop through X and Y in the following manner:

```
HPLOT A+X(1), B-Y(1)
FOR I=1 TO N
HPLOT TO A+X(I), B-Y(I)
NEXT I
```

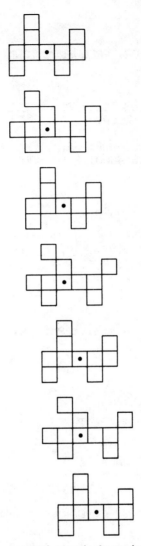

Figure 9.6   Sequence of moves in the moving dog program.

```
]LIST
5   REM   MOVING DOG PROGRAM
10    PRINT "ENTER COLOR, FREQUENCY, AND DELAY"
20    INPUT C,N,D
30    FOR I = 1 TO N
40    HOME : GR
50    X = 2:Y = 20: GOSUB 3000: REM   SETUP
60    GOSUB 4000: REM   DELAY
70    FOR X = 2 TO 36
80    GOSUB 1000: GOSUB 4000: REM   MOVE 1 AND DELAY
90    GOSUB 2000: GOSUB 4000: REM   MOVE 2 AND DELAY
100   NEXT X
110   NEXT I
120   TEXT : HOME
130   PRINT "END OF PROGRAM"
140   GOTO 9999
999   REM   MOVE 1
1000  COLOR= C: PLOT X,Y - 1: PLOT X + 3,Y - 1
1010  PLOT X - 1,Y + 1: PLOT X + 2,Y + 1
1020  COLOR= 0: PLOT X - 1,Y - 1: PLOT X + 2,Y - 1
1030  PLOT X - 2,Y + 1: PLOT X + 1,Y + 1
1040  RETURN
1999  REM   MOVE 2
2000  COLOR= C: PLOT X + 3,Y: PLOT X,Y - 2
2010  COLOR= 0: PLOT X - 2,Y: PLOT X - 1,Y - 2
2020  RETURN
2999  REM   SETUP
3000  COLOR= C
3010  HLIN X - 2,X + 2 AT Y
3020  VLIN Y - 2,Y AT X - 1
3030  PLOT X + 2,Y - 1: PLOT X - 2,Y + 1: PLOT X + 1,Y + 1
3040  RETURN
3999  REM   DELAY
4000  FOR Z = 1 TO D: NEXT Z
4010  RETURN
9999  END
```

Figure 9.7   Listing of the moving dog program demonstrating low-resolution animation.

Thus, the points are connected to form a desired image. Hence, the origin is denoted by point (A,B) and N is the number of points. Movement and speed are achieved by changing the reference point, (A,B) in the previous example, at increasing and decreasing rates of speed.

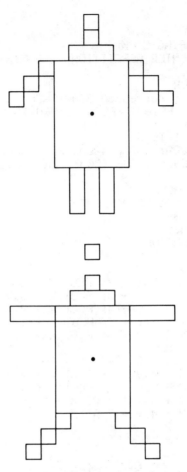

Figure 9.8 Schematic of the jumping jack program.

Illustrative Example — Racing Car Program

Figure 9.10 gives a schematic of a racing car outlined as a set of points, and Figure 9.11 gives a high-resolution graphics program designed to move the racing car along a road at increasing rates of speed. The program, of course, reads the points comprising the image into arrays, as outlined above. As suggested in the second

```
]LIST

5  REM  JUMPING JACK
10   PRINT "ENTER REPETITIONS AND TIME"
20   INPUT N,T:C = 15
30   HOME : GR
40   X = 20:Y = 20: GOSUB 3000: REM  SETUP
50   VTAB 23: PRINT "PRESS RETURN TO START": INPUT A$
60   HOME
70   FOR I = 1 TO N
80   GOSUB 1000: GOSUB 4000: REM  MOVE 1 AND DELAY
90   GOSUB 2000: GOSUB 4000: REM  MOVE 2 AND DELAY
100   NEXT I
110   TEXT : HOME
120   PRINT "END OF WORKOUT"
130   GOTO 9999
140   GOTO 9999
999   REM  JUMP UP
1000   COLOR= C
1010   PLOT X,Y - 7
1020   PLOT X - 4,Y - 3: PLOT X + 4,Y - 3
1030   PLOT X - 5,Y - 3: PLOT X + 5,Y - 3
1050   PLOT X - 2,Y + 4: PLOT X + 2,Y + 4
1060   PLOT X - 3,Y + 5: PLOT X + 3,Y + 5
1065   PLOT X - 4,Y + 6: PLOT X + 4,Y + 6
1070   COLOR= 0
1080   PLOT X,Y - 6
1090   PLOT X - 4,Y - 2: PLOT X + 4,Y - 2
1100   PLOT X - 5,Y - 1: PLOT X + 5,Y - 1
1110   VLIN Y + 4,Y + 7 AT X - 1
1120   VLIN Y + 4,Y + 7 AT X + 1
1130   RETURN
1999   REM  JUMP DOWN
2000   COLOR= C
2010   PLOT X,Y - 6
2020   PLOT X - 4,Y - 2: PLOT X + 4,Y - 2
2030   PLOT X - 5,Y - 1: PLOT X + 5,Y - 1
2040   VLIN Y + 4,Y + 7 AT X - 1
2050   VLIN Y + 4,Y + 7 AT X + 1
2060   COLOR= 0
2070   PLOT X,Y - 7
2080   HLIN X - 5,X - 4 AT Y - 3
2090   HLIN X + 4,X + 5 AT Y - 3
2100   PLOT X - 2,Y + 4: PLOT X + 2,Y + 4
2110   PLOT X - 3,Y + 5: PLOT X + 3,Y + 5
2115   PLOT X - 4,Y + 6: PLOT X + 4,Y + 6
2120   RETURN
2999   REM  SETUP
```

Figure 9.9 Listing of the jumping jack program.

```
3000   COLOR= C
3010   VLIN Y - 6,Y - 4 AT X
3020   HLIN X - 1,X + 1 AT Y - 4
3030   FOR I = Y - 3 TO Y + 3
3040   HLIN X - 2,X + 2 AT I
3050   NEXT I
3060   VLIN Y + 4,Y + 7 AT X - 1
3070   VLIN Y + 4,Y + 7 AT X + 1
3080   PLOT X - 3,Y - 3: PLOT X + 3,Y - 3
3090   PLOT X - 4,Y - 2: PLOT X + 4,Y - 2
3100   PLOT X - 5,Y - 1: PLOT X + 5,Y - 1
3110   RETURN
3999   REM  DELAY
4000   FOR Z = 1 TO T: NEXT Z
4010   RETURN
9999   END
```

Figure 9.9   (Continued)

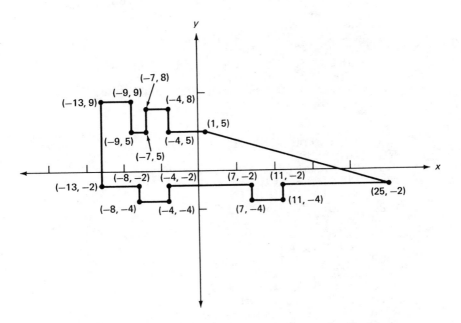

Figure 9.10   Schematic of an image constructed as a series of points.

```
]LIST

5   REM   RACING CAR
6   REM   READ FIGURE
10  READ N,T: REM   # OF PTS AND DELAY
20  DIM X(N),Y(N)
30  FOR I = 1 TO N
40  READ X(I),Y(I)
50  NEXT I
99  REM   SET GRAPHICS MODE
100  HGR
110  HCOLOR= 3
120 R = 5.6 / 7: REM   SCREEN DISTORTION
199  REM   DRAW ROAD
200  HPLOT 0,86 TO 279,86
210  REM   START CAR
220 A = 15:B = 80
230  HCOLOR= 3: GOSUB 1000: REM   DRAW CAR
240  VTAB 21
250  PRINT "ENTER SPEED AND ACCELERATION"
260  INPUT S,DS
270  REM   GO
280  FOR J = S TO 280 STEP DS
290  FOR A = 15 TO 250 STEP J
300  HCOLOR= 3: GOSUB 1000: REM   DRAW CAR
310  GOSUB 2000: REM   DELAY
320  HCOLOR= 0: GOSUB 1000: REM   ERASE CAR
330  NEXT A
340  NEXT J
350  VTAB 21
360  PRINT "END OF RACE"
370  GOTO 9999
999  REM   DRAW CAR AT PT (A,B)
1000  HPLOT A + X(1),B - Y(1)
1010  FOR I = 2 TO N
1020  HPLOT   TO A + X(I),B - Y(I)
1030  NEXT I
1040  RETURN
1999  REM   DELAY
2000  FOR Z = 1 TO T: NEXT Z
2010  RETURN
4999  REM   OUTLINE OF CAR
5000  DATA   19,50: REM   # OF PTS & DELAY
5010  DATA   25,-2,1,5,-4,5,-4,8,-7,8,-7,5,-9,5
5020  DATA   -9,9,-13,9,-13,-2,-8,-2,-8,-4
5030  DATA   -4,-4,-4,-2,7,-2,7,-4,11,-4,11,-2
5040  DATA   25,-2
9999  END
```

Figure 9.11   Listing of the racing car program.

animation principle, the illusion of speed is given by increasing the distance between successive images. Thus, in the program, the speed (S) gives the initial distance between images, and the acceleration (DS) gives the amount by which the distance is increased for each pass across the screen. Figure 9.12 gives a display of the racing car stopped in time.

VOCABULARY LIST

Knowledge of the following terms and concepts will assist the reader in becoming familiar with animated graphics:

Delay
Displacement principle
Reference point
Speed principle
(x,y) orientation

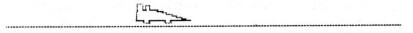

Figure 9.12   Graphic image of the racing car stopped in time.

10

Image Transformation in Small-Computer Graphics

In small computers, the term *image transformation* refers to either a translation, a rotation, or a scaling. Each of these concepts is covered in this chapter in both two-dimensional and three-dimensional environments. Some mathematics is contained in this chapter, however, the results are nontechnical in nature and can be used without full comprehension of the underlying theory. High-resolution graphics is used exclusively in image transformation.

BASIC TECHNIQUES

In order to do image transformation in small-computer graphics, it is important (or even necessary) to consider six aspects of the problem:

- Storage of an image
- Display of an image
- Projection of an image
- Translation of an image
- Rotation of an image
- Scaling of an image

Storage

Because high-resolution graphics is being employed, it is convenient to store an image as an array of points, which is subsequently displayed with a series of HPLOT commands. Transformations can then be made to the row prior to its display without obscuring the ordering relationships among the points.

Display

An array of points is displayed through the use of control information stored with the data. The control information determines whether a particular point is the first point in a chain of lines, or whether it is an intermediate point. Figure 10.1 gives the storage of a hypothetical array of points in two dimensions. The display algorithm is:

$$if \; c_i = 1 \;\; then$$
$$\text{PLOT } x_i, y_i$$

$$else$$
$$\text{PLOT TO } x_i, y_i$$

This technique is effective in image transformation since the topology of a curve is invariant under translation, rotation, and scaling.

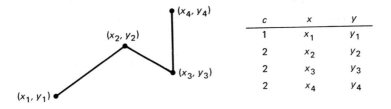

c	x	y
1	x_1	y_1
2	x_2	y_2
2	x_3	y_3
2	x_4	y_4

Figure 10.1 Storage of an array of points.

Projection

Projection of two-dimensional objects is straightforward. An (x,y) image is projected on the (x,y) plane. In three dimensions, a decision has to be made concerning the method to be used. In this chapter, a suitable method is to project a three-dimensional image on the (x,y) plane by eliding the z coordinate.

Translation

Translation of an image is the shifting of the points that comprise the image, as suggested by Figure 10.2. A trnaslation is always performed relative to the coordinate system in which the points reside. In a pure translation, the size of the image does not change.

Rotation

Rotation of an image is the shifting of the points that comprise an image around a point, as demonstrated in Figure 10.3. In many cases, rotation is performed around the origin, but this need not necessarily be the case. In three dimensions, rotation is performed with an axis orientation. The relationship between the points in rotation does not change, so the size of the image does not change.

Scaling

In the scaling of an image in small-computer graphics, a multiplicative factor is applied to each point in the image. As suggested in Figure 10.4, the size of an image can change in scaling.

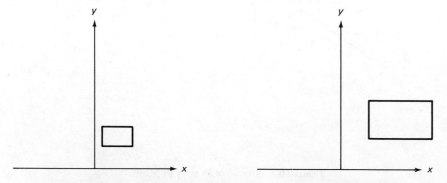

Figure 10.2   Translation of an image in two dimensions (3-D not shown).

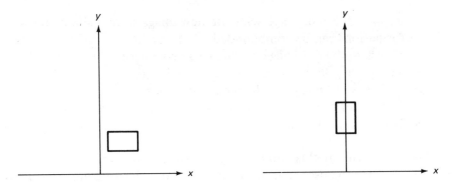

Figure 10.3   Rotation of an image about the origin in two dimensions (3-D not shown).

Method of Presentation

A unique method is used to present the subject matter. A general program has been developed for two-dimensional transformation and for three-dimensional transformation. As each topic is presented, an example is run using this general program.

TWO-DIMENSIONAL TRANSFORMATION

The two-dimensional transformation program is given in Figure 10.5. Through a carefully selected method of presentation, the following options are available:

- Read an image from the data statements. This is the "old" image.
- Plot the old image on a suitable set of axes.
- Plot a "new" image obtained through a transformation.

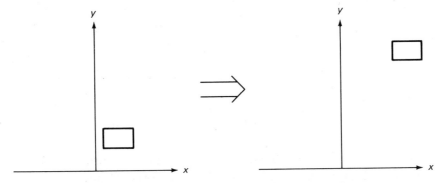

Figure 10.4   Scaling of an image in two dimensions (3-D not shown).

- Replace the old image with the new image so that simple transformations can be compounded.
- Translate the old image producing a new image.
- Rotate the old image producing a new image.
- Scale the old image producing a new image.
- Enter a set of points by hand — one by one.
- Terminate execution.

The reader can, at this point, easily follow the program as it presents a "menu" for the user to select an option, and as the program branches to a specific part of the program to perform the required function. Two of these options are illustrated in Figure 10.6, which demonstrates the READ and PLOT functions for sample data. In the following sections, the reader should attempt to identify exactly which statements perform the subject operations.

Translation

In mathematics, the translation of point (x,y) by m units in the x direction and n units in the y direction takes the form:

$$[x \ y \ 1] \begin{bmatrix} 1 & 0 & 0 \\ 0 & 1 & 0 \\ m & n & 1 \end{bmatrix} = [x^* \ y^* \ 1]$$

where the point (x^*,y^*) is the new point that has been translated. Full comprehension of the mathematics is not necessary as the above matrix equations translate to the following formulas:

$$x^* = x + m$$
$$y^* = y + n$$

and then to the following BASIC statements (lines 6710 and 6720):

X2(I)=X1(I)+M
Y2(I)=Y1(I)+N

The result of this mathematical manipulation and programming is shown in Figure 10.7, which translates the original image by 20 in the x direction and 15 in the y direction.

```
iLIST

5   REM   2D TRANSFORMATION
10   DIM C(100),X1(100),Y1(100),X2(100),Y2(100)
20  L = 1000: REM   DELAY
25  CC = 3: REM   COLOR
30   REM   PRINT MENU
50   TEXT : HOME
60   HTAB 15: PRINT "2D TRANSFORMATION": PRINT
70   PRINT "SELECT DESIRED OPTION:": PRINT
80   HTAB 10: PRINT "1   READ IMAGE"
90   HTAB 10: PRINT "2   PLOT OLD IMAGE"
100   HTAB 10: PRINT "3   PLOT NEW IMAGE"
110   HTAB 10: PRINT "4   REPLACE: OLD <- NEW"
120   HTAB 10: PRINT "5   TRANSLATE"
130   HTAB 10: PRINT "6   ROTATE"
140   HTAB 10: PRINT "7   SCALE"
150   HTAB 10: PRINT "8   ENTER PTS BY HAND"
160   HTAB 10: PRINT "9   STOP"
170   PRINT
180   PRINT "ENTER # BETWEEN 1 AND 9 INCLUSIVE"
190   INPUT A
200   IF (A < 1) OR (A > 9) THEN 180
210   REM   BRANCH TO SELECTED OPTION
220   IF A = 1 THEN 1000: REM   READ
230   IF A = 2 THEN 1500: REM   PLOT OLD
240   IF A = 3 THEN 2000: REM   PLOT NEW
250   IF A = 4 THEN 2500: REM   REPLACE OLD
260   IF A = 5 THEN 3000: REM   TRANSLATE
270   IF A = 6 THEN 3500: REM   ROTATE
280   IF A = 7 THEN 4000: REM   SCALE
290   IF A = 8 THEN 4500: REM   ENTER BY HAND
300   REM   FALL THROUGH TO STOP
310   HOME
320   PRINT "END OF PROGRAM EXECUTION"
330   END
998   REM   REM READ/DATA
1000   GOSUB 5000
1010   PRINT "READ COMPLETE"
1020   FOR I = 1 TO L: NEXT I: REM   DELAY
1030   GOTO 50
1498   REM   PLOT OLD IMAGE
1500   HGR : HCOLOR= CC
1510   GOSUB 5500: REM   DRAW AXES
1520   GOSUB 6000: REM   PLOT OLD
1530   VTAB 24
1540   PRINT "ENTER 1 WHEN FINISHED"
1550   INPUT A
1560   GOTO 50
```

Figure 10.5   Listing of the two-dimensional transformation program.

```
1998   REM   PLOT NEW
2000   HGR : HCOLOR= CC
2010   GOSUB 5500: REM   PLOT AXES
2020   GOSUB 6200: REM   PLOT NEW
2030   GOTO 1530
2498   REM   REPLACE OLD WITH NEW
2500   GOSUB 6500
2510   PRINT "REPLACEMENT COMPLETE"
2520   GOTO 1020
2998   REM   TRANSLATE
3000   HOME
3010   PRINT "ENTER X TRANSLATION"
3020   INPUT M
3030   PRINT "ENTER Y TRANSLATION"
3040   INPUT N
3050   PRINT "GOOD"
3060   GOSUB 6700
3070   PRINT "TRANSLATION COMPLETE"
3080   GOTO 1020
3498   REM   ROTATE
3500   HOME
3510   PRINT "ENTER ANGLE"
3520   INPUT AN
3530   PRINT "ENTER ROTATION POINT"
3540   INPUT "X: ";M
3550   INPUT "Y: ";N
3560   PRINT "GOOD"
3570   GOSUB 7000
3580   PRINT "ROTATION COMPLETE"
3590   GOTO 1020
3998   REM   SCALE
4000   HOME
4010   PRINT "ENTER X SCALE FACTOR"
4020   INPUT C
4030   PRINT "ENTER Y SCALE FACTOR"
4040   INPUT D
4050   PRINT "GOOD"
4060   GOSUB 7500
4070   PRINT "SCALING COMPLETE"
4080   GOTO 1020
4498   REM   ENTER BY HAND
4500   HOME
4510   PRINT "ENTER # OF POINTS"
4520   INPUT NP
4530   PRINT "ENTER C,X, AND Y UNTIL FINISHED"
4540   FOR I = 1 TO NP
4550   PRINT "PT ";I;": ";
4555   INPUT C(I),X1(I),Y1(I)
4560   NEXT I
```

Figure 10.5 (Continued)

```
4570   PRINT "INPUT COMPLETE"
4580   GOTO 1020
4998   REM   READ PTS
5000   RESTORE : READ NP
5010   FOR I = 1 TO NP
5020   READ C(I),X1(I),Y1(I)
5030   NEXT I
5040   RETURN
5498   REM   DRAW AXES
5500   HPLOT 0,80 TO 279,80
5510   HPLOT 140,0 TO 140,159
5520   RETURN
5998   REM   PLOT OLD IMAGE
6000   FOR I = 1 TO NP
6010 X = X1(I) + 140:Y = 80 - Y1(I)
6020   IF X > 279 THEN X = 279
6030   IF X < 0 THEN X = 0
6040   IF Y > 159 THEN Y = 159
6050   IF Y < 0 THEN Y = 0
6060   IF C(I) = 1 THEN 6090
6070   HPLOT   TO X,Y
6080   GOTO 6100
6090   HPLOT X,Y
6100   NEXT I
6110   RETURN
6198   REM   PLOT NEW IMAGE
6200   FOR I = 1 TO NP
6210 X = X2(I) + 140:Y = 80 - Y2(I)
6220   IF X > 279 THEN X = 279
6230   IF X < 0 THEN X = 0
6240   IF Y > 159 THEN Y = 159
6250   IF Y < 0 THEN Y = 0
6260   IF C(I) = 1 THEN   GOTO 6290
6270   HPLOT   TO X,Y
6280   GOTO 6300
6290   HPLOT X,Y
6300   NEXT I
6310   RETURN
6498   REM   REPLACE
6500   FOR I = 1 TO NP
6510 X1(I) = X2(I):Y1(I) = Y2(I)
6520   NEXT I
6530   RETURN
6698   REM   TRANSLATION
6700   FOR I = 1 TO NP
6710 X2(I) = X1(I) + M
6720 Y2(I) = Y1(I) + N
6730   NEXT I
6740   RETURN
```

Figure 10.5   (Continued)

```
6998  REM  ROTATION
7000  TH = AN / 57.3
7010  ST =  SIN (TH):CT =  COS (TH)
7020  CZ = CT - 1
7030  FOR I = 1 TO NP
7040  X2(I) = X1(I) * CT - Y1(I) * ST - M * CZ + N * ST
7050  Y2(I) = X1(I) * ST + Y1(I) * CT - M * ST - N * CZ
7060  NEXT I
7070  RETURN
7498  REM  SCALING
7500  FOR I = 1 TO NP
7510  X2(I) = C * X1(I)
7520  Y2(I) = D * Y1(I)
7530  NEXT I
7540  RETURN
8998  REM  SAMPLE DATA
9000  DATA  5
9010  DATA  1,5,5
9020  DATA  0,45,5
9030  DATA  0,45,25
9040  DATA  0,5,25
9050  DATA  0,5,5
```

Figure 10.5   (Continued)

Rotation

In mathematics, the rotation point (x, y) about the point (m, n) through the angle takes the form:

$$[x \quad y \quad 1] \begin{bmatrix} 1 & 0 & 0 \\ 0 & 1 & 0 \\ -m & -n & 1 \end{bmatrix} \begin{bmatrix} \cos\theta & \sin\theta & 0 \\ -\sin\theta & \cos\theta & 0 \\ 0 & 0 & 1 \end{bmatrix} \begin{bmatrix} 1 & 0 & 0 \\ 0 & 1 & 0 \\ m & n & 1 \end{bmatrix} = [x^* \quad y^* \quad 1]$$

where, as before, the point (x^*, y^*) is the new point that has been put through the following sequence of geometric operations:

- Translation by $(-m, -n)$
- Rotation by θ through the origin
- Translation by (m, n) to its original position

The above matrix equations translate to the following formulas:

$$x^* = x \cos\theta - y \sin\theta - m(\cos\theta - 1) + n \sin\theta$$
$$y^* = x \sin\theta + y \cos\theta - m \sin\theta - n(\cos\theta - 1)$$

```
]RUN
                    2D TRANSFORMATION

SELECT DESIRED OPTION:

         1   READ IMAGE
         2   PLOT OLD IMAGE
         3   PLOT NEW IMAGE
         4   REPLACE: OLD <- NEW
         5   TRANSLATE
         6   ROTATE
         7   SCALE
         8   ENTER PTS BY HAND
         9   STOP

ENTER # BETWEEN 1 AND 9 INCLUSIVE
?1
READ COMPLETE
                    2D TRANSFORMATION

SELECT DESIRED OPTION:

         1   READ IMAGE
         2   PLOT OLD IMAGE
         3   PLOT NEW IMAGE
         4   REPLACE: OLD <- NEW
         5   TRANSLATE
         6   ROTATE
         7   SCALE
         8   ENTER PTS BY HAND
         9   STOP

ENTER # BETWEEN 1 AND 9 INCLUSIVE
?2
ENTER 1 WHEN FINISHED
```

Figure 10.6 Illustration of the two-dimensional READ and PLOT operations for sample data.

```
                    2D TRANSFORMATION

SELECT DESIRED OPTION:

              1   READ IMAGE
              2   PLOT OLD IMAGE
              3   PLOT NEW IMAGE
              4   REPLACE: OLD <- NEW
              5   TRANSLATE
              6   ROTATE
              7   SCALE
              8   ENTER PTS BY HAND
              9   STOP

ENTER # BETWEEN 1 AND 9 INCLUSIVE
?5
ENTER X TRANSLATION
?20
ENTER Y TRANSLATION
?15
GOOD
TRANSLATION COMPLETE
                    2D TRANSFORMATION

SELECT DESIRED OPTION:

              1   READ IMAGE
              2   PLOT OLD IMAGE
              3   PLOT NEW IMAGE
              4   REPLACE: OLD <- NEW
              5   TRANSLATE
              6   ROTATE
              7   SCALE
              8   ENTER PTS BY HAND
              9   STOP

ENTER # BETWEEN 1 AND 9 INCLUSIVE
?3
ENTER 1 WHEN FINISHED
```

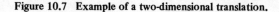

Figure 10.7   Example of a two-dimensional translation.

and then to the following BASIC statements (lines 7010, 7020, 7040, and 7050):

ST=SIN (TH) : CT=COS (TH)
CZ=CT-1
X2 (I)=X1 (I) *CT-Y1 (I) *ST-M*CZ+N*ST
Y2 (I)=X1 (I) *ST+Y1 (I) *CT-M*ST-N*CZ

The result of this mathematical manipulation and programming is shown in Figure 10.8, which rotates the original image by $180°$ about the point $(0,0)$.

Scaling

In mathematics, the scaling of point (x, y) by a factor of c in the x direction and d in the y direction takes the form:

$$[x \quad y \quad 1] \begin{bmatrix} c & 0 & 0 \\ 0 & d & 0 \\ 0 & 0 & 1 \end{bmatrix} = [x^* \quad y^* \quad 1]$$

where the point (x^*, y^*) is the new point that has been scaled. The above matrix equations translate to the following formulas:

$$x^* = cx$$
$$y^* = dy$$

and then to the following BASIC statements (lines 7510 and 7520):

X2 (I)=C*X1 (I)
Y2 (I)=D*Y1 (I)

The result of this mathematical manipulation and programming is shown in Figure 10.9, which scales the original image by two in the x direction and three in the y direction.

```
                    2D TRANSFORMATION

SELECT DESIRED OPTION:

          1   READ IMAGE
          2   PLOT OLD IMAGE
          3   PLOT NEW IMAGE
          4   REPLACE: OLD <- NEW
          5   TRANSLATE
          6   ROTATE
          7   SCALE
          8   ENTER PTS BY HAND
          9   STOP

ENTER # BETWEEN 1 AND 9 INCLUSIVE
?6
ENTER ANGLE
?180
ENTER ROTATION POINT
X: 0
Y: 0
GOOD
ROTATION COMPLETE
                    2D TRANSFORMATION

SELECT DESIRED OPTION:

          1   READ IMAGE
          2   PLOT OLD IMAGE
          3   PLOT NEW IMAGE
          4   REPLACE: OLD <- NEW
          5   TRANSLATE
          6   ROTATE
          7   SCALE
          8   ENTER PTS BY HAND
          9   STOP

ENTER # BETWEEN 1 AND 9 INCLUSIVE
?3
ENTER 1 WHEN FINISHED
```

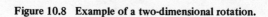

Figure 10.8 Example of a two-dimensional rotation.

```
                 2D TRANSFORMATION

SELECT DESIRED OPTION:

             1   READ IMAGE
             2   PLOT OLD IMAGE
             3   PLOT NEW IMAGE
             4   REPLACE: OLD <- NEW
             5   TRANSLATE
             6   ROTATE
             7   SCALE
             8   ENTER PTS BY HAND
             9   STOP

ENTER # BETWEEN 1 AND 9 INCLUSIVE
?7
ENTER X SCALE FACTOR
?2
ENTER Y SCALE FACTOR
?3
GOOD
SCALING COMPLETE
                 2D TRANSFORMATION

SELECT DESIRED OPTION:

             1   READ IMAGE
             2   PLOT OLD IMAGE
             3   PLOT NEW IMAGE
             4   REPLACE: OLD <- NEW
             5   TRANSLATE
             6   ROTATE
             7   SCALE
             8   ENTER PTS BY HAND
             9   STOP

ENTER # BETWEEN 1 AND 9 INCLUSIVE
?3
ENTER 1 WHEN FINISHED
```

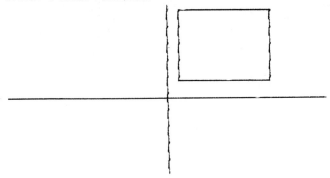

Figure 10.9   Example of a two-dimensional scaling.

THREE-DIMENSIONAL TRANSFORMATION —
A PICTORIAL APPROACH

While image transformation is interesting, at least from a mathematical point of view, the preceding section was a bit complicated for a non-technical introduction to small-computer graphics. As it turns out, three-dimensional transformations are even more complicated.

In order to develop a program for three-dimensional transformation, it was necessary to get into the mathematics. However, there is no reason why everyone should delve into that level of detail. As an alternate approach to mathematics, this section gives a pictorial approach to three-dimensional graphics. The subject matter is presented as a scenario of three-dimensional transformation. First, a short note on the axes and method of projection is necessary.

Figure 10.10 gives a view of the coordinate axes in three dimensions. The computer program displays the x, y plane as points are projected on it. Thus, a cube may appear as a square until it is transformed.

As the user looks at the screen in three-dimensional graphics, the view is from the z axis.

Figure 10.11 through 10.19 give a pictorial walkthrough of three-dimensional transformation.

VOCABULARY LIST

Knowledge of the following terms and concepts will assist the reader in becoming familiar with the subject of image transformation:

Control information
Image transformation
Projection
Rotation
Scaling
Translation

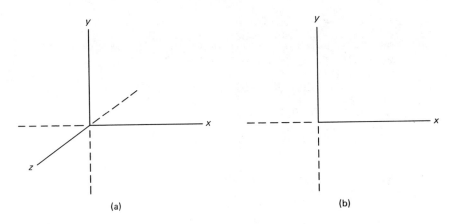

Figure 10.10   Coordinate axes for three-dimensional graphics.

```
]LIST

5   REM    3D TRANSFORMATION
10   DIM C(50),X1(50),Y1(50),X2(50),Y2(50),Z1(50),Z2(50)
20  L = 1000: REM   DELAY
25  CC = 3: REM   COLOR
30   REM   PRINT MENU
50   TEXT : HOME
60   HTAB 10: PRINT "3D TRANSFORMATION": PRINT
70   PRINT "SELECT DESIRED OPTION:": PRINT
80   HTAB 10: PRINT "1   READ IMAGE"
90   HTAB 10: PRINT "2   PLOT OLD IMAGE"
100   HTAB 10: PRINT "3   PLOT NEW IMAGE"
110   HTAB 10: PRINT "4   REPLACE: OLD <- NEW"
120   HTAB 10: PRINT "5   TRANSLATE"
130   HTAB 10: PRINT "6   ROTATE"
140   HTAB 10: PRINT "7   SCALE"
150   HTAB 10: PRINT "8   ENTER PTS BY HAND"
160   HTAB 10: PRINT "9   STOP"
170   PRINT
180   PRINT "ENTER # BETWEEN 1 AND 9 INCLUSIVE"
190   INPUT A
200   IF (A < 1) OR (A > 9) THEN 180
210   REM   BRANCH TO SELECTED OPTION
220   IF A = 1 THEN 1000: REM   READ
230   IF A = 2 THEN 1500: REM   PLOT OLD
240   IF A = 3 THEN 2000: REM   PLOT NEW
250   IF A = 4 THEN 2500: REM   REPLACE OLD
260   IF A = 5 THEN 3000: REM   TRANSLATE
```

Figure 10.11 Listing of the three-dimensional graphics program. Note similarity between this and the 2-D program, and also that each operation is implemented as a GOSUB subroutine.

```
270   IF A = 6 THEN 3500: REM   ROTATE
280   IF A = 7 THEN 4000: REM   SCALE
290   IF A = 8 THEN 4500: REM   ENTER BY HAND
300   REM   FALL THROUGH TO STOP
310   HOME
320   PRINT "END OF PROGRAM EXECUTION"
330   END
998   REM   REM READ/DATA
1000  GOSUB 5000
1010  PRINT "READ COMPLETE"
1020  FOR I = 1 TO L: NEXT I: REM   DELAY
1030  GOTO 50
1498  REM   PLOT OLD IMAGE
1500  HGR : HCOLOR= CC
1510  GOSUB 5500: REM   DRAW AXES
1520  GOSUB 6000: REM   PLOT OLD
1530  VTAB 24
1540  PRINT "ENTER 1 WHEN FINISHED"
1550  INPUT A
1560  GOTO 50
1998  REM   PLOT NEW
2000  HGR : HCOLOR= CC
2010  GOSUB 5500: REM   PLOT AXES
2020  GOSUB 6200: REM   PLOT NEW
2030  GOTO 1530
2498  REM   REPLACE OLD WITH NEW
2500  GOSUB 6500
2510  PRINT "REPLACEMENT COMPLETE"
2520  GOTO 1020
2998  REM   TRANSLATE
3000  HOME
3010  PRINT "ENTER X TRANSLATION"
3020  INPUT M
3030  PRINT "ENTER Y TRANSLATION"
3040  INPUT N
3050  PRINT "ENTER Z TRANSLATION"
3060  INPUT P
3070  PRINT "GOOD"
3080  GOSUB 6700
3090  PRINT "TRANSLATION COMPLETE"
3100  GOTO 1020
3498  REM   ROTATE
3500  HOME
3502  PRINT "ENTER AXES: X->1, Y->2, Z->3
3504  INPUT AX
3506  IF (AX < 1) OR (AX > 3) THEN 3502
3510  PRINT "ENTER ANGLE"
3520  INPUT AN
3530  PRINT "ENTER ROTATION POINT"
```

Figure 10.11 (Continued)

```
3540   INPUT "X: ";M
3550   INPUT "Y: ";N
3555   INPUT "Z: ";P
3560   PRINT "GOOD"
3570   GOSUB 7000
3580   PRINT "ROTATION COMPLETE"
3590   GOTO 1020
3998   REM   SCALE
4000   HOME
4010   PRINT "ENTER X SCALE FACTOR"
4020   INPUT C
4030   PRINT "ENTER Y SCALE FACTOR"
4040   INPUT D
4042   PRINT "ENTER Z SCALE FACTOR"
4044   INPUT E
4050   PRINT "GOOD"
4060   GOSUB 7500
4070   PRINT "SCALING COMPLETE"
4080   GOTO 1020
4498   REM   ENTER BY HAND
4500   HOME
4510   PRINT "ENTER # OF POINTS"
4520   INPUT NP
4530   PRINT "ENTER C, X, Y, AND Z"
4540   FOR I = 1 TO NP
4550   PRINT "PT ";I;": ";
4555   INPUT C(I),X1(I),Y1(I),Z1(I)
4560   NEXT I
4570   PRINT "INPUT COMPLETE"
4580   GOTO 1020
4998   REM   READ PTS
5000   RESTORE : READ NP
5010   FOR I = 1 TO NP
5020   READ C(I),X1(I),Y1(I),Z1(I)
5030   NEXT I
5040   RETURN
5498   REM   DRAW AXES
5500   HPLOT 0,80 TO 279,80
5510   HPLOT 140,0 TO 140,159
5520   RETURN
5998   REM   PLOT OLD IMAGE
6000   FOR I = 1 TO NP
6010   X = X1(I) + 140:Y = 80 - Y1(I)
6020   IF X > 279 THEN X = 279
6030   IF X < 0 THEN X = 0
6040   IF Y > 159 THEN Y = 159
6050   IF Y < 0 THEN Y = 0
6060   IF C(I) = 1 THEN 6090
6070   HPLOT   TO X,Y
```

Figure 10.11   (Continued)

```
6080  GOTO 6100
6090  HPLOT X,Y
6100  NEXT. I
6110  RETURN
6198  REM  PLOT NEW IMAGE
6200  FOR I = 1 TO NP
6210 X = X2(I) + 140:Y = 80 - Y2(I)
6220  IF X > 279 THEN X = 279
6230  IF X < 0 THEN X = 0
6240  IF Y > 159 THEN Y = 159
6250  IF Y < 0 THEN Y = 0
6260  IF C(I) = 1 THEN  GOTO 6290
6270  HPLOT  TO X,Y
6280  GOTO 6300
6290  HPLOT X,Y
6300  NEXT I
6310  RETURN
6498  REM  REPLACE
6500  FOR I = 1 TO NP
6510 X1(I) = X2(I):Y1(I) = Y2(I):Z1(I) = Z2(I)
6520  NEXT I
6530  RETURN
6698  REM  TRANSLATION
6700  FOR I = 1 TO NP
6710 X2(I) = X1(I) + M
6720 Y2(I) = Y1(I) + N
6725 Z2(I) = Z1(I) + P
6730  NEXT I
6740  RETURN
6998  REM  ROTATION
7000 TH = AN / 57.3
7010 ST =  SIN (TH):CT =  COS (TH)
7020  IF AX = 1 THEN 7120
7030  IF AX = 2 THEN 7180
7040  REM  Z-AXIS
7050  FOR I = 1 TO NP
7060 X2(I) = (X1(I) - M) * CT - (Y1(I) - N) * ST + M
7070 Y2(I) = (X1(I) - M) * ST + (Y1(I) - N) * CT + N
7080 Z2(I) = Z1(I)
7090  NEXT I
7100  RETURN
7110  REM  X-AXIS
7120  FOR I = 1 TO NP
7130 X2(I) = X1(I)
7140 Y2(I) = (Y1(I) - N) * CT - (Z1(I) - P) * ST + N
7150 Z2(I) = (Y1(I) - N) * ST + (Z1(I) - P) * CT + P
7160  NEXT I
7170  RETURN
7180  REM  Y-AXIS
```

Figure 10.11   (Continued)

```
7190  FOR I = 1 TO NP
7200  X2(I) = (X1(I) - M) * CT + (Z1(I) - P) * ST + M
7210  Y2(I) = Y1(I)
7220  Z2(I) =  - (X1(I) - M) * ST + (Z1(I) - P) * CT + P
7230  NEXT I
7240  RETURN
7498  REM  SCALING
7500  FOR I = 1 TO NP
7510  X2(I) = C * X1(I)
7520  Y2(I) = D * Y1(I)
7525  Z2(I) = E * Z1(I)
7530  NEXT I
7540  RETURN
9798  REM  SAMPLE DATA
9800  DATA  16
9802  DATA  1,10,50,10
9804  DATA  0,50,50,10
9806  DATA  0,50,10,10
9808  DATA  0,10,10,10
9810  DATA  0,10,50,10
9812  DATA  0,10,50,40
9814  DATA  0,50,50,40
9816  DATA  0,50,50,10
9818  DATA  0,50,50,40
9820  DATA  0,50,10,40
9822  DATA  0,50,10,10
9824  DATA  0,50,10,40
9826  DATA  0,10,10,40
9828  DATA  0,10,10,10
9830  DATA  0,10,10,40
9832  DATA  0,10,50,40
```

Figure 10.11   (Continued)

```
]RUN
           3D TRANSFORMATION

SELECT DESIRED OPTION:

           1  READ IMAGE
           2  PLOT OLD IMAGE
           3  PLOT NEW IMAGE
           4  REPLACE: OLD <- NEW
           5  TRANSLATE
           6  ROTATE
           7  SCALE
           8  ENTER PTS BY HAND
           9  STOP

ENTER # BETWEEN 1 AND 9 INCLUSIVE
?1
READ COMPLETE
           3D TRANSFORMATION

SELECT DESIRED OPTION:

           1  READ IMAGE
           2  PLOT OLD IMAGE
           3  PLOT NEW IMAGE
           4  REPLACE: OLD <- NEW
           5  TRANSLATE
           6  ROTATE
           7  SCALE
           8  ENTER PTS BY HAND
           9  STOP

ENTER # BETWEEN 1 AND 9 INCLUSIVE
?2
ENTER 1 WHEN FINISHED
```

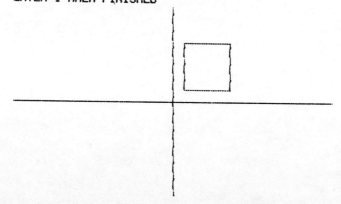

Figure 10.12 Initiation of the three-dimensional transformation program execution and display of the image − a cube in this case − on the *x, y* plane.

```
          3D TRANSFORMATION

SELECT DESIRED OPTION:

          1   READ IMAGE
          2   PLOT OLD IMAGE
          3   PLOT NEW IMAGE
          4   REPLACE: OLD <- NEW
          5   TRANSLATE
          6   ROTATE
          7   SCALE
          8   ENTER PTS BY HAND
          9   STOP

ENTER # BETWEEN 1 AND 9 INCLUSIVE
?6
ENTER AXES: X->1, Y->2, Z->3
?2
ENTER ANGLE
?45
ENTER ROTATION POINT
X: 0
Y: 0
Z: 0
GOOD
ROTATION COMPLETE
          3D TRANSFORMATION

SELECT DESIRED OPTION:

          1   READ IMAGE
          2   PLOT OLD IMAGE
          3   PLOT NEW IMAGE
          4   REPLACE: OLD <- NEW
          5   TRANSLATE
          6   ROTATE
          7   SCALE
          8   ENTER PTS BY HAND
          9   STOP

ENTER # BETWEEN 1 AND 9 INCLUSIVE
?4
REPLACEMENT COMPLETE
```

Figure 10.13 Rotation of the image at 45° about the *y* axis and replacement of the old image storage area with the rotated object.

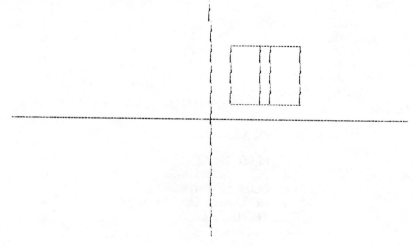

```
        3D TRANSFORMATION

SELECT DESIRED OPTION:

        1  READ IMAGE
        2  PLOT OLD IMAGE
        3  PLOT NEW IMAGE
        4  REPLACE: OLD <- NEW
        5  TRANSLATE
        6  ROTATE
        7  SCALE
        8  ENTER PTS BY HAND
        9  STOP

ENTER # BETWEEN 1 AND 9 INCLUSIVE
?2
ENTER 1 WHEN FINISHED
```

Figure 10.14 Display of the cube after being rotated at 45° about the *y* axis. Note: the 3-D effect does not yet show because of the projection.

```
        3D TRANSFORMATION

SELECT DESIRED OPTION:

        1  READ IMAGE
        2  PLOT OLD IMAGE
        3  PLOT NEW IMAGE
        4  REPLACE: OLD <- NEW
        5  TRANSLATE
        6  ROTATE
        7  SCALE
        8  ENTER PTS BY HAND
        9  STOP

ENTER # BETWEEN 1 AND 9 INCLUSIVE
?6
ENTER AXES: X->1, Y->2, Z->3
?1
ENTER ANGLE
?-45
ENTER ROTATION POINT
X: 0
Y: 0
Z: 0
GOOD
ROTATION COMPLETE
        3D TRANSFORMATION

SELECT DESIRED OPTION:

        1  READ IMAGE
        2  PLOT OLD IMAGE
        3  PLOT NEW IMAGE
        4  REPLACE: OLD <- NEW
        5  TRANSLATE
        6  ROTATE
        7  SCALE
        8  ENTER PTS BY HAND
        9  STOP

ENTER # BETWEEN 1 AND 9 INCLUSIVE
?4
REPLACEMENT COMPLETE
```

Figure 10.15 Rotation of the cube at -45° about the *x* axis and replacement of the old image with the new image.

```
        3D TRANSFORMATION

SELECT DESIRED OPTION:

        1  READ IMAGE
        2  PLOT OLD IMAGE
        3  PLOT NEW IMAGE
        4  REPLACE: OLD <- NEW
        5  TRANSLATE
        6  ROTATE
        7  SCALE
        8  ENTER PTS BY HAND
        9  STOP

ENTER # BETWEEN 1 AND 9 INCLUSIVE
?2
ENTER 1 WHEN FINISHED
```

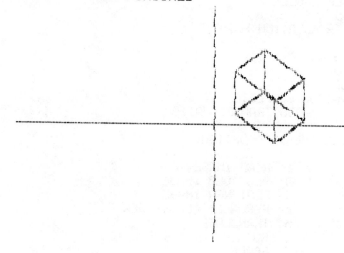

Figure 10.16 Display of the cube after the x axis rotation.

```
        3D TRANSFORMATION

SELECT DESIRED OPTION:

        1   READ IMAGE
        2   PLOT OLD IMAGE
        3   PLOT NEW IMAGE
        4   REPLACE: OLD <- NEW
        5   TRANSLATE
        6   ROTATE
        7   SCALE
        8   ENTER PTS BY HAND
        9   STOP

ENTER # BETWEEN 1 AND 9 INCLUSIVE
?5
ENTER X TRANSLATION
?25
ENTER Y TRANSLATION
?25
ENTER Z TRANSLATION
?0
GOOD
TRANSLATION COMPLETE
        3D TRANSFORMATION

SELECT DESIRED OPTION:

        1   READ IMAGE
        2   PLOT OLD IMAGE
        3   PLOT NEW IMAGE
        4   REPLACE: OLD <- NEW
        5   TRANSLATE
        6   ROTATE
        7   SCALE
        8   ENTER PTS BY HAND
        9   STOP

ENTER # BETWEEN 1 AND 9 INCLUSIVE
?4
REPLACEMENT COMPLETE
```

Figure 10.17   Translation of the cube by (25,25,0) and replacement of the old image.

```
3D TRANSFORMATION

SELECT DESIRED OPTION:

       1   READ IMAGE
       2   PLOT OLD IMAGE
       3   PLOT NEW IMAGE
       4   REPLACE: OLD <- NEW
       5   TRANSLATE
       6   ROTATE
       7   SCALE
       8   ENTER PTS BY HAND
       9   STOP

ENTER # BETWEEN 1 AND 9 INCLUSIVE
?2
ENTER 1 WHEN FINISHED
```

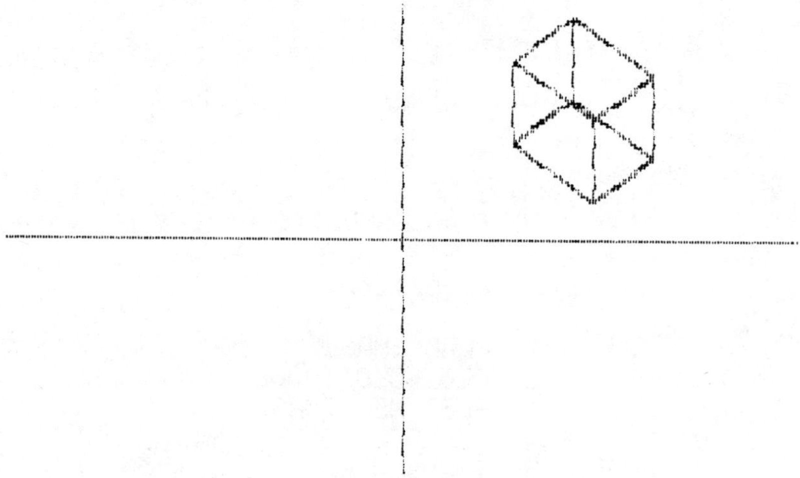

Figure 10.18   Display of the cube after the translation of (25,25,0).

3D TRANSFORMATION

SELECT DESIRED OPTION:

          1   READ IMAGE
          2   PLOT OLD IMAGE
          3   PLOT NEW IMAGE
          4   REPLACE: OLD <- NEW
          5   TRANSLATE
          6   ROTATE
          7   SCALE
          8   ENTER PTS BY HAND
          9   STOP

ENTER # BETWEEN 1 AND 9 INCLUSIVE
?7
ENTER X SCALE FACTOR
?.5
ENTER Y SCALE FACTOR
?.5
ENTER Z SCALE FACTOR
?2
GOOD
SCALING COMPLETE
          3D TRANSFORMATION

SELECT DESIRED OPTION:

          1   READ IMAGE
          2   PLOT OLD IMAGE
          3   PLOT NEW IMAGE
          4   REPLACE: OLD <- NEW
          5   TRANSLATE
          6   ROTATE
          7   SCALE
          8   ENTER PTS BY HAND
          9   STOP

ENTER # BETWEEN 1 AND 9 INCLUSIVE
?3
ENTER 1 WHEN FINISHED

Figure 10.19   Scaling of the cube by (0.5, 0.5, 2) and display of the result.

References

Applesoft BASIC Programming Reference Manual. Cupertino, California: Apple Computer, Inc., 1978, Form #A2L0006.

Beeten, J., "Vector graphics for raster displays," *Byte* (October, 1980), pp. 286–293.

Bleher, J. H., et al., "A graphic interactive application monitor," *IBM Systems Journal,* Volume 19, Number 3 (1980), pp. 382–402.

Bliss, F. W., and G. M. Hyman, "Selecting and implementing a turnkey graphics system," *Computer Graphics and Applications,* Volume 1, Number 2 (April, 1981), pp. 55–70.

Brown, B. E., and S. Levine, "The future of computer graphics," *Byte* (November, 1980), pp. 22–28.

Burchi, R. S., "Interactive graphics today," *IBM Systems Journal,* Volume 19, Number 3 (1980), pp. 292–313.

Cesa, L., "Kinetic string art for the Apple," *Byte* (November, 1980), pp. 63–63.

Crow, F. C., "Three-dimensional computer graphics, Part 1," *Byte* (March, 1981), pp. 54–82.

Crow, F. C., "Three-dimensional computer graphics, Part 2," *Byte* (April, 1981), pp. 290–302.

Gardner, T., "Selecting a stroke graphics system by architecture," *Mini-Micro Systems* (December, 1979), pp. 94–98.

George, J. E., "Computer graphics and the business executive – the new management team," *Computer Graphics and Applications,* Volume 1, Number 1 (January, 1981), pp. 57–71.

Handelman, S. W., "A high-resolution computer graphics system," *IBM Systems Journal,* Volume 19, Number 3 (1980), pp. 356–366.

Hobbs, L. C., "Computer graphics display hardware," *IEEE Computer Graphics and Applications,* Volume 1, Number 1 (January, 1981), pp. 25–39.

Inman, D., *Introduction to TRS-80 Graphics.* Portland, Oregon: Dilithium Press, 1979.

Katzan, Harry, *Introduction to Computers and Data Processing*. New York: D. Van Nostrand Company, 1979.

Kelley, N. D., "Computer graphics: Info at a glance," *Inforsystems* (December, 1979), pp. 37–39.

Lerner, E. J., "Fast graphics use parallel techniques," *IEEE Spectrum*, Volume 18, Number 3 (March, 1981), pp. 34–38.

Loceff, M., "A new approach to high-speed computer graphics: the line," *Computer*, Volume 13, Number 6 (June, 1980), pp. 56–66.

Machover, C., M. Neighbors, and C. Stuart, "Graphics displays," *IEEE Spectrum* (August, 1977), pp. 24–32.

Machover, C., M. Neighbors, and C. Stuart, "Graphics displays: factors in systems design," *IEEE Spectrum* (October, 1977), pp. 23–27.

Machover, C., "Computer graphics in the 80s," *Mini-Micro Systems* (December, 1979), pp. 80–84.

Machover, C., "A guide to sources of information about computer graphics," *Computer Graphics and Applications*, Volume 1, Number 1 (January, 1981), pp. 73–85.

McManigal, D. F., and D. A. Stevenson, "Architecture of the IBM 3277 graphics attachment," *IBM Systems Journal*, Volume 19, Number 3 (1980), pp. 331–344.

Myers, W., "Computer graphics: the human interface," *Computer*, Volume 13, Number 6 (June, 1980), pp. 45–54.

Myers, W., "Computer graphics: Reaching the user," *Computer*, Volume 14, Number 3 (March, 1981), pp. 7–14.

Niehoff, W. H., and A. L. Jones, "An APL approach to presentation graphics," *IBM Systems Journal*, Volume 19, Number 3 (1980), pp. 367–381.

Orr, J., "Interactive computer graphics systems," *Mini-Micro Systems* (December, 1979), pp. 68–78.

Rogers, D. F., and J. A. Adams, *Mathematical Elements for Computer Graphics*. New York: McGraw-Hill Book Company, 1976.

Schmucker, K., "The mathematics of computer art," *Byte* (July, 1979), pp. 105–116.

Shepherd, B. J., "Experimental page makeup of text with graphics on a raster printer," *IBM Systems Journal*, Volume 19, Number 3 (1980), pp. 345–355.

Sokol, D., and J. Shepard, "Three-dimensional graphics for the Apple II," *Byte* (November, 1980), pp. 148–154.

Stiefel, M. L., "Color hard copy for graphics applications," *Mini-Micro Systems* (January, 1980), pp. 104–107.

Taylor, M. W., "Color CRT terminals gain wider popularity," *Mini-Micro Systems* (December, 1979), pp. 86–90.

The Applesoft Tutorial. Cupertino, California: Apple Computer, Inc., 1979, Form #A2L0018.

Wadsworth, N., *Introduction to Low Resolution Graphics*. Elmwood, Connecticut: Scelbi Publications, 1979.

Waite, M., *Computer Graphics Primer*. Indianapolis: Howard W. Sams and Company, Inc., 1979.

Watson, A., "A simplified theory of video graphics, Part 1," *Byte* (November, 1980), pp. 180–189.

Watson, A., "A simplified theory of video graphics, Part 2," *Byte* (December, 1980), pp. 142–156.

Weller, D. L., et al., "Software architecture for graphical interaction," *IBM Systems Journal,* Volume 19, Number 3 (1980), pp. 314–330.

Appendix: Syntactical Conventions

Most programmers recognize that the process of constructing a computer program is a creative act and that once a program is suitably encoded, it is as much a contribution to the world of knowledge as a poem, a mathematical formula, or an artist's sketch. In fact, computer programming is regarded by some as an art rather than a science. A computer program written in a programming language becomes a body of knowledge when a description of that language is available that can be used to distinguish between a syntactically valid program and a syntactically invalid program and to determine the meaning of the program. A language that describes another language is called a *metalanguage,* and most programming languages utilize a set of syntactical conventions of this kind.

The most frequent use of a metalanguage is to describe a statement in a programming language in a way that allows the reader to construct a valid instance of a particular statement. Thus, the metalanguage should utilize a notation outside of the programming language being described by a user of the language described.

The metalanguage used in this book employs seven rules and appropriate symbols, given as follows:

1. A *notation variable* names a constituent of a programming language. It takes one of two forms: (1) lowercase letters, digits, and hyphens — beginning with a letter; for example:

> constant
> arithmetic-variable
> date-name-1

or (2) two or more words separated by hyphens where one word consists of lowercase letters and the others consist of uppercase letters. For example:

> DATA-statement
> MAT-READ-statement
> MOVE-statement

A notation variable represents information that must be supplied by the user and is defined formally or informally in preceding or adjacent text.

2. A *notation constant* stands for itself and is represented by capital letters or by special characters. A notation constant must be written as shown. For example:

> GOSUB statement-number
> NEXT arithmetic-variable
> PROCEDURE DIVISION.

In this statement, the words GOSUB, NEXT, and PROCEDURE DIVISION are notation constants and must be written as indicated.

3. A *syntactical unit* is a notation variable, a notation constant, or a collection of notation variables, notation constants, and notation symbols enclosed in braces and brackets.

4. The *vertical bar* | is read "or" and indicates that a choice must be made between the item to the left of the bar and the item to the right of the bar. For example:

> character-reference | arithmetic-reference
> &PI | *E | *SQE2

5. A set of *braces* is used for grouping or to indicate that a choice is to be made among the syntactical units contained in the braces. For example:

> {+ | -}
> {integer-constant | fixed-point constant}

Alternately, the syntactical units may be stacked vertically within the braces. For example:

> {identifier-1}
> {literal   }

6. A set of *brackets* [ ] represents an option and indicates that the enclosed syntactical units can be omitted. For example:

> [+ | -]
> alphabetic-character [numeric-character]

Alternately, the optional syntactical units may be stacked vertically within the brackets. For example:

> {RIGHT}
> {LEFT }

7. The *ellipsis* (a series of three periods) indicates that the preceding syntactical unit may be repeated one or more times. For example:

> DATA constant [, constant] . . .
>
> MOVE {identifier-1} TO identifier-2 [identifier-3]
>   {literal   }

The syntactical conventions can be further illustrated by some examples from the BASIC and COBOL languages. The *FOR statement* in BASIC has the form:

FOR arithmetic-variable=arithmetic-expression TO
arithmetic-expression [STEP arithmetic-expression]

An example of this FOR statement is:

FOR I=J TO M/2 STEP 2

The *IF statement* in COBOL has the form:

IF condition $\begin{Bmatrix} \text{statement-1} \\ \text{NEXT SENTENCE} \end{Bmatrix}$ ELSE $\begin{Bmatrix} \text{statement-2} \\ \text{NEXT SENTENCE} \end{Bmatrix}$

An example of the IF statement is:

IF AGE>40 MOVE 'EKG TEST' TO CREMK ELSE ALL 1 TO LCOUNT.

Index